MOCK THE WEEK

BRAND SPANKING NEW SCENES WE'D LIKE TO SEE

MOCK THE WEEK

BRAND SPANKING NEW SCENES WE'D LIKE TO SEE

Ewan Phillips, Dan Patterson, Simon Bullivant,
Rob Colley, Dan Gaster, Ged Parsons, Giles Pilbrow,
Steve Punt and Colin Swash

BOXTREE

First published 2014 by Boxtree
an imprint of Pan Macmillan, a division of Macmillan Publishers Limited
Pan Macmillan, 20 New Wharf Road, London N1 9RR
Basingstoke and Oxford
Associated companies throughout the world
www.panmacmillan.com

ISBN 978-1-4472-6963-2

1 3 5 7 9 8 6 4 2

A CIP catalogue record for this book is available from the British Library.

Printed and bound by CPI Group (UK) Ltd, Croydon, CR0 4YY

MOCK THE WEEK

BRAND SPANKING NEW SCENES WE'D LIKE TO SEE

UNLIKELY THINGS FOR
A VET TO SAY

'Good news! I managed to cut your pet lizard free from that weird bowl he'd got himself trapped in . . . oh, your pet *tortoise*?'

'I've injected your hamster with adrenalin. Not for health reasons, but we've had a power cut, and him going round that wheel is our only hope of generating any electricity.'

'It's an unusual injury for this sort of animal – your snail's got whiplash.'

'I'm afraid we've run out of goldfish bowls, so I've put Goldie into this liquidizer, where he'll be . . . DON'T TOUCH THAT SWITCH!'

'I see that your two dogs are called Marks and Spencer – oh, that's right, they're a pair of boxers.'

'I'm sorry to say that Timmy needs a new set of hips – and that's quite a major operation for a tarantula.'

'First, I'm going to remove this leg . . . give it back to the postman . . . and then I'm going to put your dangerous Rottweiler to sleep.'

'I'm afraid I'm going to put your horse down – he's far too heavy, and he's making my arms ache.'

'I meant "put the dog down *on the chair*".'

'Good news, Doctor, just two patients left to see, the python and the white mouse . . . no, just the python.'

'Nice try, Mrs Henderson, I'm not putting him down. I can see it's just your father-in-law with fur stuck on him.'

'Do you want Rover's body back? Only he'd look great as a rug in front of my fire.'

'The operation on the pit bull's stomach was a success and we've managed to get the face back out.'

'It says on the form that you're married, Madam, yet you've brought in six cats with you.'

'The results are back in from your pet rabbit. Apparently it was delicious.'

'I *know* that it's technically a hamster, but if you want it removed from *there* you need to go to casualty.'

'This badger has been gassed. That's because Ratty had the three-bean salad.'

'I've flushed little Goldie down the lavatory – it's not easy getting a Labrador round the U-bend, but I did manage it in the end.'

UNLIKELY THINGS TO READ
IN AN OBITUARY

A LOVING FATHER, AND VERY NEARLY THE WORLD RECORD
HOLDER FOR THE LONGEST JUMP BETWEEN TWO BUILDINGS.

HE NEVER MARRIED, AS HE PREFERRED SHAGGING AN
ENDLESS STREAM OF MODELS.

DAVID DICKINSON'S FUNERAL WAS YESTERDAY. THE COFFIN WAS
LOWERED INTO THE GROUND; SIX FEET LONG, HEAVILY VARNISHED
AND MAHOGANY . . . DAVID WILL BE SORELY MISSED.

A LOVING MOTHER, GRANDMOTHER, GREAT-GRANDMOTHER
AND GREAT-GREAT-GRANDMOTHER. GONE TOO SOON.

OLIVER REED WILL BE CREMATED AT THREE O'CLOCK
THIS AFTERNOON, AND IS EXPECTED TO GO OUT
SOMETIME NEXT TUESDAY.

LOVING WIFE, AND SISTER, OF BRIAN. WITH LOVE FROM
ALL IN NORWICH.

NOT DEAD, BUT SLEEPING, AT THE WHEEL OF THE TRUCK.
THEN DEAD.

NOT DEAD, BUT SLEEPING. BUT WE BURIED HIM ANYWAY.

GONE BUT NOT FORGOTTEN: GEORGE . . . UM, GEORGE . . .
IT'S ON THE TIP OF MY TONGUE . . .

GONE! HE'S GONE. THOSE BLOODY GRAVE-ROBBERS.

BAD THINGS TO SAY AT CUSTOMS

'I hear you can't bring meat into this country. What am I going to do with this eighteen inches in my pants?'

'Occupation? Not sure how to describe it, really. . . I'll just put "The Jackal".'

'Stick your hand up my arse? Ha! Yeah? You and whose army? . . . Oh, them.'

'Eh? I thought you could take heroin in, if it was under 100ml?'

'Yes, I have got something to declare. I declare you are a wanker.'

'Excuse me – if my cocaine is from Europe, do I go through the blue channel?'

'Oh, get a real job, you perv.'

'Smuggling something in? No, you are! Terrorist? Look who's talking!'

'OK – it begins with S, it's up my arse, and it rhymes with "hemtex".'

'I don't know how long I'll be here. I just have instructions to meet a man called Kerim in a hotel lobby, and await orders from the Ayatollah.'

'Did I pack these bags? *Nein*, I voz helped by der Führer.'

AN UNLIKELY GUIDE TO
KEEPING TROPICAL FISH

For a special treat, pour a smoothie slowly into the fish tank. They love that.

However much you feel you want to – and you will often feel this urge – try not to get into the bowl with the goldfish.

Pages 77–649: Recipes

If the fish gets bigger than the tank, then you need to stop feeding it.

Fish love to be taken out of the water occasionally and stroked.

One good, solid name for a fish is Edward. It is unpretentious and will give it confidence for life.

One good way to give your fish proper exercise is to take it to the local swimming baths two or three times a week.

Try to discourage bad habits by forbidding your fish to sleep in a bed with you. If it must be in the bedroom, then let it sleep in the false-teeth mug.

Training your fish is difficult, and requires diligence and hours of patience. If it refuses to cooperate, take it out of the water until it changes its mind.

Always address your fish as 'ma'am', or at least 'she'. A fish is not an 'it'.

Try to encourage your male fish to swim around a lot to let off steam. Female fish should be guided into areas of domestic usefulness such as cooking, cleaning or flower-arranging.

If a fin falls off, just glue it back. Your fish will thank you in the long run.

When it comes to fish, no means no.

Some of my happiest afternoon walks have been with my fish in tow.

In an emergency, most fish are of little help. Make plans that don't include them.

One way to monitor your fish's progress is to give it weekly tests.

Fish have very short memories, so buying them gifts and doing them favours are of little, if any value.

They may be old wives' tales, but some old rhymes contain a lot of sense: 'Fish, fish, clean them out, the less you do the more they shout, the more they pout the less they'll do and soon you'll be flushing them down the loo'.

Don't keep your fish just for yourself. Show people how much you love them – and I don't just mean by balancing them on your penis.

If your fish are getting too frisky, put the bowl in the freezer. There's nothing better to cool the little bastards down.

UNLIKELY THINGS TO HEAR
IN HOSPITAL

'The penis is looking rather swollen; I'll put it away, shall I, Nurse, and go and examine the patient.'

'OK then, Captain Birdseye: open wide and say "Arrrrrrrr".'

'Well, Mr Inverdale, good news – I think we've managed to get Marion Bartoli's tennis racquet out of your arse.'

'Well, we've operated on your scrotum, Mr Jagger . . . what? That's his face?'

'Enjoy your stay in hospital. And remember to keep a supply of pound coins on you at all times – the beds are on a meter now.'

'Mr Gascoigne, that sanitizing wash is for cleaning your hands, not drinking.'

'Well, Mr Jones, we had to remove ten feet of your lower intestine. The important thing now is that you keep fit – what are you like at skipping?'

'OK, nurses, as your teacher this is possibly the best piece of advice I can ever give you: "Milk, milk, lemonade, round the corner, chocolate's made".'

'Let's just do this smear test. I can see you've had quite a few children, Mrs Smith . . . ith . . . ith . . . ith. Echo! . . . echo . . . echo . . .'

'As part of Bring Your Child to Work Day, little Keith will be preparing your colonoscopy.'

BAD TITLES FOR MEMOIRS

Froome with a View – Not Very Exciting Photos Taken by Britain's Best Cyclist Off His Bike

Westlife – The Autobiography of Fred and Rose West

Argie Bargie – Diego Maradona Takes a Narrowboat Holiday through Britain's Historic Canals and Waterways

Farage Sale by Nigel Farage

Fred and Ginger – Footballing Tales from Brazilian Striker Fred and His Old Mucker Paul Scholes

The Heighway Code – The Story of Former Liverpool and Ireland Winger Steve Heighway

The Science of Sleep – An Examination of Dancer Wayne Sleep

Drawing a Blank – Various Portraits of Former Lloyds Chairman Sir Victor Blank

Gerrard's Cross – The Liverpool and England Midfielder Reveals His Frustration at the 2013–14 Season

A Thousand Splendid Sons – The Story of Britain's Most Prolific Sperm Donor

These Boots Were Made for Walken – The Memories of Hollywood's Finest Cobbler

Batt 'n' Berg – More Adventures with 'The Wombling Song' Writer Mike Batt and Norwegian Central Defender Henning Berg

Kenneth Clarke Ha Ha Ha! – All the Finest Jokes from the Roly-Poly Tory Grandee

Alliss in Wonderland – Golf Thoughts from the BBC's Veteran Commentator, while Taking Mescaline

Hideous Fat Paedophile – The Cyril Smith Story

A Brief History of Thyme by Delia Smith

A Lovely Lovely Lad – The George Galloway Story

The Silence of the Lambs – Former England Cricketer Allan Lamb and *Place in the Sun* star Amanda Lamb spend a month in a Trappist monastery

I Did It My Wahey by Eric Morecambe

UNLIKELY THINGS TO HEAR ON A BUSINESS PROGRAMME

'The interest rate has plummeted, but that's what happens when you watch a boring business programme.'

'So, Dragons, that's the design for my new calculator. I would like [*taps figures into calculator*] thrumpty-five pounds for eleventy-two per cent of the business.'

'Time for our feature on junk Bonds. That George Lazenby wasn't much good.'

'Put your shoes back on, Susan. That's it from the Footsie.'

'Time for a discussion on the latest Euro problem: it stings when I pee.'

'Brian has come on *Dragons' Den* to pitch a TV show about four dead-eyed, grumpy millionaires.'

'Fred is trying to impress the Dragons with his design for a sawn-off shotgun, and he seems to have got the £100,000 he was after.'

'Can you send the candidates in now . . . can you send the cand . . . can you . . . bloody Amstrad machines.'

'So that's a double whammy for pensioners struggling with the dilemma of "Heat or Eat", as there's been a massive increase in the price of gas *and* cat food.'

'Now for the latest from the door furniture company "Knobs and Knockers", who have offered a profits warning, despite getting millions of hits on the Internet.'

'And remember: the valuc of shares may go down, as well as plummet.'

'Once again it was a rocky day for the pound, largely due to those c**ts in the banking world.'

'Unfortunately, Stephanie Flanders has left us to take up a highly paid job in the city. But don't worry, we've still got Robert Peston, and he's promised to start wearing thigh-high leather boots too.'

'OK, Dragons, here's my pitch. It's a TV show in which a bunch of smarmy, ruthless, rich pricks sit in judgement over desperate, poor morons for the public's gratification.'

UNLIKELY SMALL ADS

FOR SALE: sail. Sale!

Are you looking for a cure for your gullibility?
Send your bank details to . . .

We offer cut-price liposuction. Also, wanted:
second-hand vacuum cleaner.

FOR SALE: two tons of three-eyed fish.
Apply the Fukushima Sardine Company, Japan.

Come to Britain's biggest umbrella market.
Indoors if wet.

MISSING CAT: old grey tabby, totally deaf,
answers to nothing.

Have you seen my missing dog? If not, do you
want a job fetching my slippers and newspaper?

Do you want a newborn puppy? Buyer collects.
Hurry down to the canal, I reckon you've got
about ten minutes.

Horse for sale. Will make lovely pet. Or lasagne.

Fickle eight-year-old, will swap red scarf for
light blue.

Escort available by the hour – or, if you want
something bigger, a Mondeo.

Live under the flight path? We'll fix the holes in your roof caused by falling frozen stowaways.

Make a date with other people who wear lenses: contact Contact Contacts.

Brand new club. Pole dancing, £10; Albanian dancing, £3.50.

Had a baby in the last few weeks? Buy a unique gift of a newspaper from the day it was born. Comes with other newspapers from that week, plus empty milk cartons and takeaway containers.

FOR SALE: bagpipes. Any offer accepted. Please contact my neighbour.

WANTED: chef to produce Waldorf salad. Apples, walnuts, grapes. Celery negotiable.

FOR SALE: mug with slogan, 'World's Greatest Dad'. No longer needed, as kids have been taken into care.

Amusing book for sale: 'How To Make Crank Calls'. To order, phone the number below and ask for Mike Hunt.

FOR SALE: John Lennon's widow. £10 ONO.

TIPS ON WORKPLACE ETIQUETTE

Learn names, and learn them quickly. Failing that, try and remember people with your own personal aide-memoire, such as 'Taffy', 'Tits', 'Fatso' or 'Wanker'.

Don't fall asleep, EVER – unless your job is really f**king boring.

Arrive early to work every day. This gives you a chance to rifle through everyone's stuff, read their emails and have a sh*t in peace.

Remember, everyone is important – even those numpties who do the admin, or those weird foreigners who clean out your bins for no money.

Never say in an email anything you wouldn't say to someone's face, unless they're bigger than you.

Remember, there is no global work day: hours vary from country to country. However, as you are British, it is up to foreigners to fit in with your life. Feel free to ring them whenever is convenient.

Don't arrive more than five minutes early for a meeting in someone else's office. They might be having a wank.

Always reply to an email or phone call within 24 hours, even if it is to tell them to f**k off.

Allways make shore that you're grammer and speling are tottaly accurate orr people is going to think you ain't got no idea what you is talking about.

Don't interrupt people, bec . . . Sorry, what did you say?

Always stand straight, turn towards people and make eye contact when they are speaking. This should help intimidate them.

When meeting someone for the first time, be sure to shake hands palm to palm, firmly but gently . . . that's it . . . ooh, keep doing that, faster, faster . . .

There is a time and a place for confrontation, and that is almost never in a meeting. It is in the toilets afterwards, using whatever weapon is at hand.

How you treat people says a lot about you. Do you hear me, you useless c**t?

Sexism is a danger. Always try and avoid making comments on a female co-worker's appearance, even if you know the little popsy would love it.

If your boss criticizes your work, request feedback as to where you could improve and always defer to their opinion. Then wank in their coffee.

Make a habit of saying, 'please', 'thank you' and 'you're welcome', e.g. 'Please make me a cup of tea, then f**k off. Thank you. You're welcome.'

Always be kind to older colleagues. They might be dead soon, and you could take their job.

It is extremely rude to arrive late for a meeting. It is ruder still to fart, scratch your balls and put your feet on the desk saying, 'Who's brewing up?' when you do get there.

If you are in the wrong, always apologize. You have plenty of time to make your colleague's life hell in the coming years.

UNLIKELY THINGS TO HEAR IN PRISON

'How thoughtful – a bucket of chocolate mousse in the corner of the cell.'

'Can I just have a poster of Rita Hayworth and a small rock hammer, please?'

'Where's my toothpaste? Honestly, it's full of bloody criminals in here.'

'Charles Bronson? Is he that big fat hairy ponce sat over there on his own?'

'Could I have a Times and an alarm call in the morning, please?'

'Adventurous? Well, I always say try anything once.'

'I can't sleep without my little fluffy bunnykins.'

'I'm only in for shoplifting, but I'm actually the Cornish Ripper.'

'Rangers or Celtic? I think they're both equally awful to be honest.'

'Hey! Why don't we all do a dance to a Michael Jackson song, like they do in the Philippines? I'll choreograph!'

'I remember when it was . . . it was about a week after I murdered that old widow . . . Sh*t.'

'I say, is it really necessary for you to keep reading aloud from your Koran?'

'Bend over so you can scrub my back? Why, that's incredibly helpful of you.'

'Well, I used to be a policeman, then a prison officer. And then I only went and got banged up on these pesky paedophilia charges.'

'Norman Stanley Fletcher . . . you're over here, on the sex offenders' wing.'

'Oh, are you the bloke who's getting a pardon? . . . April Fool! Ha ha!'

'I'd like to use my time in prison to explore my sexuality.'

'Guard! Guard! There's a hole in my cell leading to the outside world!'

'I'd like Chicken Provençal, cream of celeriac, raspberry coulis . . .'

'I'm sorry, "Cruncher", but the Feng Shui is all wrong in this cell.'

UNLIKELY SEXTING

'I'm not wearing any underwear . . . because my arse is really chapped and flaking.'

'Here is a picture of my cock. By the way, whose number is this?'

'Let me take you to a place I know called Orgasmland . . . it's just behind the bins in the Lidl car park.'

'Squirt your juice in me . . . that is, if you can poke your tiny white straw in my little silver hole.'

'I've been a bad girl today, and I need to be punished. I've cleaned out your bank account and strangled your cat.'

'OMG. Left in such a rush today, I kinda forgot to wear a bra . . . luv, Colin.'

'That tie you're wearing . . . let's use it tonight . . . the pipe in the airing cupboard is dripping.'

'I had a dream about you and it was "18"! I know I'm 42, which makes it a bit creepy.'

'Do you like what you see? Yeah? Good, because it's really hard! Thanks for giving my equations the once-over, Miss, see you in class in the morning.'

'Something is missing today. Can I come and look for it up your arse?'

'Can you add something to your to-do list today . . . me? Yeah? Oh, and get some bog roll, teabags, cat litter, a tin of creosote and some more of that fungal foot powder of mine from the chemist's.'

'I've just taken off my knickers. They've got a bit skiddy.'

'I was just thinking about you in the shower . . . I was thinking, it's now four weeks since you promised you'd fix that crack in the shower head.'

'I want to be naughty with you in the office. Let's hide all last month's accounts.'

'Whenever you touch me, I start to throb everywhere . . . it must be an allergy. Have you been eating shellfish?'

'Want to scream all night tonight? Pop by mine, we're infested by mice.'

'Thanks to you, I no longer need porn . . . you've completely turned me off scx.'

'You have taught me how to make love to a man, and I thank you. Now can we actually do it, rather than sitting in a classroom with a flip chart?'

'I want to rip your clothes off and lick every part of you. Apart from your feet – they're f**king repulsive.'

'I can't concentrate. I just keep looking at your bulge . . . you should really get that looked at, it can't be right.'

BAD TITLES FOR MEMOIRS

Tim Brooke-Taylor, Soldier, Spy – The Chirpy Goodie's War Years

David Moyes: The United ~~Years~~ ~~Year~~ Ten Months

My Life (Well, Not Including the Last 18 Months or So) by Stuart Hall

The Greatest Cape and Other Misprints by Steve McQueen

East of Eden – Memories of Living Near the Former Prime Minister Sir Anthony Eden

Murphy's Law – Ex England Midfielder Danny Murphy's Hilarious Tales from England's Small Claims Courts

Come On, Remember the Good Stuff by Rolf Harris

What I Did on My Birthday by Yaya Touré

Electoral Success My Way by Nick Clegg

I Capture the Castle – The Very Best Photos of Former Record Breakers Presenter Roy Castle

BAD THINGS TO SEE ON SOCIAL MEDIA

You have a message from 'Operation Yewtree'.

Based on your searches, posts and friends, Facebook has worked out an individual profile tailored to you! Turns out you're a c**t.

Edward Snowden has tagged you in a list of US spies operating in world trouble spots.

You have three requests to post your holiday photos to WankedIn, the best online network for sneaky masturbation over candid snaps of people you know a bit.

'RT Here is an Instagram pic from my Facebook album, "Stuff I put on Snapchat". Follow my tumblr blog, "I Am Never F**king Offline".'

Welcome to YoungBieberFans. Which lorry driving firm do you work for?

Vladimir Putin wants to be your 'friend'.

Jason Manford, Vernon Kay and Ashley Cole liked your photo.

I'm sending you a seven-second video of my cock on Snapchat. This will be the longest I have ever had sex for.

Crimewatch UK have added your picture to their album, 'Rogue's Gallery: Do You Know Their Whereabouts?'

I got Stuart Hall! Take this quiz and find out which 1970s celebrity you are!

Buzzfeed's Top 10 Videos of Cats that Every Single Woman Should Send to Her Friends.

Prince Harry read the *Bild* article 'Die Arse der Kate Middleton' 359 times.

David Moyes added Ryan Giggs to the group 'Failed Manchester United Managers'.

Prince Charles thought Elizabeth II might be interested in the article 'King Juan Carlos Abdicates'.

Welcome to Google Plus, the social networking site where we already know everything there is to know about you before you join.

MySpace and Friends Reunited sent you a message on quill and parchment saying, 'Whither art thou?'

Welcome to China's biggest social networking site. Make friends, share photos and videos and get an extra thrill from worrying your posts will result in prison, death and the site being shut down.

I am clicking off MyLife. Goodbye, cruel world!

BAD THINGS TO HEAR WHEN SITTING DOWN ON THE TOILET

[*Whispers*] 'And here, for the very first time on
Life on Earth, rare HD footage of a middle-aged man
curling one out.'

Something swimming up from the bowl

'What do you think of the new chili-pepper toilet roll,
Bernard?'

'Surpriiiiissse!'

'Oi! Oi! Turn FaceTime off quick, for f**k's sake.'

The doorbell

Your testicle getting trapped in the seat

'Psst . . . mate, over here, the little hole halfway down.'

A pig grunting

The unmistakable rattle of an empty toilet-roll holder

'Tonight, This Is Your Life.'

'Hello, fancy meeting you here.'

'Fire!'

'Say cheese!'

'Jesus! What is that bloody smell?'

'OK: nobody try anything, and you'll all get out of here in one piece.'

'Remember not to use the toilet, it's not plumbed in.'

'At last! I've been hanging around aeroplane toilets for fifty years waiting to join the Mile High Club.'

'Is there anybody in there? I'm Nick Clegg, and I'd like to talk to you about Europe.'

'And let's go live to our camera now to see someone having a sh*t.'

'Excuse me, sir, this is the Harrods bathroom showroom – you can't do that there.'

'Toilet roll commercial, take 2, and . . . ACTION!'

'Hey! That isn't a toilet – it's a well, covered by a very weak old plank.'

'Surprise, surprise! I'm Holly Willoughby.'

'Sorry to bother you, but I'm a gastroenterologist in the next cubicle, and you really don't sound good. Do you mind if I examine you?'

'That isn't toilet paper – it's Semtex!'

'I'm sorry, that isn't a toilet. It is a chair, and you are on *Mastermind*.'
'I know – but I've started, so I'll finish.'

'Here's my homework, sir.'

'Yesssss! What a goal! England have scored and won the World Cup!'

'Stop! I'm already sitting here, you blind bastard.'

'Run! The volcano's erupting!'

'Ha ha! You fell for my plan: that seat has been booby-trapped to go off with any sudden movement.'

'Has anyone seen my pet anaconda?'

'The gunman is hiding in one of those cubicles. We can't take any chances. Torch the lot.'

'We will now leave the Space Station, Houston. Blast off is in ten seconds.'

BAD TAGLINES FOR MOVIES

Gladiator – starring Omid Djalili from ITV's *Splash* and *In the Night Garden*'s Sir Derek Jacobi

Schindler's List – If your name's not down . . .

First Blood – Monosyllabic tramp massively overreacts

Lord of the Rings – Let's be honest . . . it's a load of bollocks

. . . Starring Robin Williams with a beard, so don't bother

Well, clearly she only did this part to get an Oscar

There Will Be Blood – You Will Be Bored

The Red Balloon – Yeah, but when all's said and done, it is just a f**king balloon

The Sixth Sense – He's dead and stuff

One Flew Over the Cuckoo's Nest – You don't have to be mad to be in this, but . . .

UNLIKELY THINGS TO HEAR
AT THE WINTER OLYMPICS

'And the bad news here is that the skeleton bob has been held up by a woman pissing about on a tea tray – oh, hang on: that is the skeleton bob.'

'Ah. There appears to have been an unfortunate misunderstanding here in Sochi: when I said earlier that both British snowboarders were "out", Russian authorities took them away to be shot.'

'Oh no, the British have put grit on the bobsleigh run!'

'And after ripping the other competitors to shreds, the grizzly bear stands alone in the grandstand.'

'Winter sports really are for everyone – it doesn't matter which public school you went to.'

'I'm afraid there's been a ski-by shooting at the biathlon.'

'And the British ski-jumper has gone so far off course, he's been eaten by Uruguayan plane crash survivors from 1972.'

'Here in Russia, now and then you catch glimpse of a beaver: that's the beauty of commentating on the ice dance.'

'F**k, this is boring.'

'Ooh, I say, look at the arse crack on that bobsleigh girl.'

'Now let's see if all that training on a grassy field in Kent has helped Britain's skiers.'

'Vladimir Putin there, on the Mardi Gras float as it enters the Pride parade.'

'No surprises today: gold for the Americans, and a Frenchman pushed in at the ski lift.'

'At last, an event the British can dominate: the après-ski.'

'And now let's have a look at the bloody Torvill and Dean *Boléro* routine yet again.'

'That's not a good start, as the British skier asks if he can go down the green run.'

'A world-beating display from the British team – that is magnificent. That's what I call a snowman!'

'I've got no idea why he's stopped. Ooh . . . hang on – the snow's turning yellow.'

'The British skier doing his traditional warm-up for the downhill – a pint of Glühwein and a bowl of spaghetti.'

'The Inuit have fifty different words for the phrase "Pointless Sporting Competition".'

BAD ADVICE FOR MEDICAL SELF-DIAGNOSIS

If it's throbbing and red, rub ointment on it immediately, although caution is needed if it belongs to someone else.

If it comes out faster than gravity would normally allow, then there's something wrong.

If it's throbbing and pink, rub cream in gently . . . yes, that's good, oh yeah, just like that, yeah . . . no, don't stop, come back . . . I was kidding . . . we could settle this privately . . . ooh, sh*t.

Contrary to popular belief, pus-filled sores on your mouth and penis are a good sign. A GOOD sign. Yep.

Quick! Check! Has your heart stopped? If yes: PANIC!

Good vomit just kind of comes out; bad vomit goes a lot further.

Try to learn some medical terminology so that you can communicate clearly and quickly with a doctor or receptionist. Useful phrases include 'pissing blood', 'driving the porcelain bus' and 'pebble-dashing the toilet'.

It is always helpful and comforting to go through a checklist in a crisis; e.g., can you pull it out? How far up is it? What will you tell your parents?

BAD THINGS FOR A NEW ENGLAND FOOTBALL MANAGER TO SAY

'Hello, my name's Steve McClaren.'

'Are you still allowed to shag all the secretaries?'

'So, remind me, is Wayne Rooney a striker or a defender?'

'Hello, I'm Kevin Keegan.'

'Right, listen up. I'm going to build the team round Darren Bent.'

'Well, yes, they were a very physical outfit, but then what do you expect? These people are savages.'

'Well, you can tell the fans they can f**k off.'

'Hello, I err Fabio Capello.'

'Disabled people are basically paying for all the sins in their past lives.'

'Can we play in black? It's so much more slimming.'

UNLIKELY NAMES FOR RACEHORSES

FIFTY SHADES OF SH*T

COMING OUT BOTH ENDS

TAXI DRIVER GROUPIE

DEATH TO THE WEST

FLAMBOYANT BIRDWATCHER

SMOULDERING PAEDO

GOT THE PAINTERS IN

BUS STOP DRINKER

SULTRY BANK MANAGER

PLAYFUL GRAVE ROBBER

UNLIKELY THINGS TO HEAR IN PRISON

'Can I read you this sonnet I've written?'

'Keep it to yourself, but I haven't really done anything.
I'm an undercover policeman.'

'They must think a lot of me – I'm in the cell used by
Harold Shipman and Fred West.'

'What's this large penis-sized hole between our two bunks for?'

'Dr Lecter? Here's your new cellmate.'

'Hello. I'm Chris Huhne. Let me talk to you about the EU.'

'You're the fourth cellmate I've had this year. Coincidentally,
the others all violently stabbed themselves to death multiple
times in their sleep. What are the odds?'

'No, get down, the rooftop protest is tomorrow.'

'Mr Clifford, I'm a mass-murdering psychopath, I want you
to improve my profile in the newspapers, or I'll kill you.'

'Isn't jail inspiring? "Yet each man kills the thing he loves,
by each let this be heard . . ." I take it you're familiar with
Wilde's 'Reading Gaol'? Allow me to read it to you.'

'Great news. They've brought back the death penalty, and
it's going to be retroactive.'

'Hello. I'm your new cellmate, Skull Cracker.'

'Me and my fellow mullahs have decided to make an example of you.'

'Wake up, wake up, the tumbril is here to transport you to Tyburn.'

'Eton Mess? No, that was the "Wankpot".'

'What do you mean, this isn't a pampered prison? You can have massages, stand-up shows, vigorous workouts and sex on tap . . . admittedly all supplied by your cellmate, Gary.'

'I like your posters. Are you a breast man, then? Good. I'm very much a bum man, if you catch my drift.'

'Don't worry, we're not all lesbians in here! I'm a necrophile.'

'Welcome to Prison Radio and our increasingly star-studded line-up . . .'

'The warders' woodwork project is really picking up pace. If I didn't know better, I'd say it was a giant set of gallows.'

'I couldn't help noticing your arse while we were showering. It really is a work of art.'

'Well, we've had our vote, and you'll be delighted to hear you have been elected this year's bitch.'

BAD NAMES FOR NEW BOYBANDS

PUBELESS

IVF

BACKDOOR BOYS

BULLSH*T

THE COALITION

BARELY LEGAL

DISCHARGE

MANSHAFT

BRISTOL TEMPLE MEADS

FISTED

BACK, SACK AND CRACK

TCP

CROQUE MONSIEUR

YOUNG, GIFTED AND BELGIAN

DOGGERS

THE 1922 COMMITTEE

WANK WANK WANK

DIARRHOEA

LEHMAN BROTHERS

RILLINGTON PLACE

TIPS ON WORKPLACE ETIQUETTE

If there is conflict, don't get personal. Let the fat, talentless c**t know what you feel in a more subtle way that even someone as thick as him can understand.

Nobody likes an office know-all! As you're probably aware, this was proved in a survey commissioned by a leading insurance company in Australia in 2008.

Remember: if you own a football club that has just won the Premier League and you are paying your star player £240,000 a week plus bonuses, don't forget to get him a cake on his birthday. This is VERY important.

If you must light a fire, use a clean piece of floor and keep it away from your colleagues' legs. When you leave at night, piss on it to ensure it has gone out.

If someone upsets you, don't let it fester. Get it out in the open. Sh*t on their desk. That way you both know where you stand and can act accordingly.

A great way to keep your colleagues amused and relaxed is to sit with your trousers down. It really is hilarious.

Bosses are softer and more vulnerable than they seem. One good tip is to continually sneak into their office and put your arm round them. They'll love that.

Try and liven the atmosphere up by surprising people. For example, when a colleague wants to give you a peck on the cheek, go for a Frenchie.

A great way of bonding with (most) of your workmates is to find a company scapegoat and make their life a misery by blaming them for everything that goes wrong. Make sure they are smaller and weaker than you.

In my opinion, you just can't talk about bodily functions – or your cock – too much.

If someone asks you for a match, always say, 'Yes. Your face, my arse,' as this never stops being funny – particularly if the asker is ugly or deformed in some way.

Once, or maybe twice, per week, run into the office and screech, 'You're all f**kwits! I hate you!' until everyone laughs. This may take a while, but is worth persevering with. If it doesn't work, try carrying a gun for maximum effect.

Breaking the ice with someone should not involve hitting them with an ice pick. This confuses some people.

If you're going away on holiday, always trash the office before leaving.

Groping has become a bit of a dirty word these days, but that doesn't mean you should cut it out completely. Just use it judiciously. Remember: everything in moderation.

A good tip to make friends is to keep 'forgetting' your lunch and then taking food from your colleagues. They will really appreciate your feedback on what their food choices would have tasted like.

BAD TAGLINES FOR MOVIES

Yes, you do get to see her tits

Amelie – If you're a middle-class ponce, you have to watch this. By law

Big – Operation Yewtree: the Movie

Anchorman – Yes, OK, it's quite funny

The Man Who Would Be King – *The Prince Charles Story*

A Nightmare on Elm Street – Just think what he's doing to the house prices

Monsieur Hulot's Holiday – Like Mr Bean, but French (no, come back! Please!)

The Philadelphia Story – The History of Cream Cheese

Das Boot – Like a good sausage: long, hard and German

Total Recall – Suddenly, he remembers, it was a really bad idea to remake this film

UNLIKELY INSTRUCTIONS FOR PAINTBALLING

Paintballing is a great way of bonding for office colleagues; equally, it can provide an outlet for simmering workplace tensions to spill over into victimization and violence.

OK, you're preparing for your paintballing session. Put on your goggles. OK, now put on the rest of your clothes.

If you are shot in a game, you are out, so you can't fire your gun. Stay on the field, or run after the shooter yelling, 'You f**king arsehole!', attempting to hit them with your weapon.

No Diving, Bombing or Heavy Petting.

Paintballing is like sex: it's fast, it's messy and, if done properly, it could leave you walking funny.

Great positions to get the best shots at your opponents include book depositories or a grassy knoll.

We always insist that you have to be at least thirteen years old to join in with our fun. As for the paintballing, you can be any age.

Stay with your team . . . unless they're really sh*t.

DO: think of an excuse not to come.

DON'T: blame me if you have a sh*t time.

It may seem like a good idea to dive around and flip over like in a Hollywood movie, but you'll just look like a massive c**t.

UNLIKELY TV LISTINGS

6.00   **Good Morning Britain** Not one of
             Susanna Reid's days today, so have a lie-in.

9.15   **One Dead Every Minute** The latest
             goings-on with the staff of Sowerberry and
             Sons, funeral directors in Grimsby.

10.00   **Have I Got a Terrible Line-Up For You**
             Worst ever episode of the topical news quiz,
             as rail delays see Ian and Paul joined at the
             last minute by ex-West Brom defender Liam
             Ridgewell and Fatboy from *Eastenders*.
             Barry 'Cillit Bang' Scott is guest host.

10.30   **The Postmen** Ian is struggling to get a big
             parcel through the letterbox. Ken has a bit of
             a dicky tummy, and has taken the day off.

11.25   **Celebrity Heir Hunters** This week, the
             family of Nelson Mandela squabble over the
             complicated division of his estate.

12.00   **Caught Red-Handed** Ha! We can see you,
             you know. You thought you'd get away with
             it because everyone has gone out and you
             could nip in the shower straight after.
             You dirty bastard.

1.00 **Top of the Pops: The 1970s** Great music from a great decade. (NB: Recently re-edited on the advice of Scotland Yard so that virtually none of the presenters or acts can be seen any more.)

2.00 **Man vs Booze** On a rainy Tuesday afternoon, Trevor attempts to drink 30 cans of Special Brew in a sparse, cold Travelodge room just off the A1.

2.45 **You Actually Have Been Framed** Harry Hill helps wrongfully convicted criminals to prove their convictions are unsafe by recovering vital CCTV footage hidden from the jury.

3.30 **24 Hours in A&E** . . . Which is why I haven't had time to do proper TV listings. I only went in with a bloody cut finger, as well.

4.30 **Horrible Histories** A celebrity panel try to work out the name of a well-known Operation Yewtree suspect by looking at what Internet material they've been viewing on their laptops.

5.00 **Four in a Bed** Don't bother. Nothing like as exciting as it sounds, it's just a load of old couples that look like they smell, slagging off each other's B&Bs.

6.00   **Spare Slot** Kept free in case James Corden has anything he wants us to put out.

6.30   **Dimbleby Dares** After the success of his tattoo, the plummy frontman gets a genital piercing and goes dogging on the South Downs.

7.00   **The One Show** In a world exclusive, Barack Obama, Bashar al-Assad and Vladimir Putin are live in the studio with Alex and Matt to discuss car insurance tips and welly wanging, and to help judge the viewer hedgehog photo competition.

7.30   **Masterchef: The Prisoners** As the fourth week of heats begins, a nervous Michel Roux and visibly perspiring Gregg Wallace supply three Category A inmates with seven ingredients and abundant rubber cutlery, and ask them very nicely to try and make a dish.

8.00   **McIntyre Undercover** In a hideous yet grimly watchable mix-up, smiley, skipping observational comic Michael McIntyre is mistakenly tasked with infiltrating a violent drugs gang in south Manchester.

8.30 **Sh*t Box** Members of the public take it in turns to go into a grey box, have a sh*t and then emerge to talk about it with Mariella Frostrup and a panel of academics.

9.00 **Slightly Less Grand Designs** In a 'Northern special', a clearly disillusioned Kevin McCloud visits Wigan to see if Colin and Doreen are still on target to complete their lean-to pigeon coop on time and under budget.

10.00 **Googlebox** Opinionated members of the public are filmed in the comfort of their own homes talking about the pornography they are downloading and viewing using a well-known search engine.

11.00 **Meet the Russians** Shock as Sergei is found dead in mysterious circumstances in his Chelsea home. Vitalya goes on a shopping spree and comes back with two Rolls-Royces, a Picasso and West Ham United. Igor enjoys a tense meal with Andrei and his strange chemical vials at Yo Sushi.

11.50 **Drugs, Sex and Suspicious Parents** Weeping parents are forced at gunpoint to watch footage of their children, away from home for the first time, attempting to smuggle drugs through international checkpoints or being trafficked.

BAD THINGS FOR A NEW ENGLAND FOOTBALL MANAGER TO SAY

'Hello, I am Sven Göran Eriksson.'

'My plan? We sign Germans and Brazilians.'

'Last one in the bath has to soap the rest of us down!'

'What do you mean, I can't pick Bale and Ramsey?
Are you trying to tell me Wales isn't in England?'

'OK, split up for five-a-side – blacks against whites.'

'Allow me to introduce you to my assistant,
Paul Gascoigne.'

'Hello. I'm Graham Taylor.'

'When we're abroad, who do I get to share a
room with?'

'When do I get to meet Faria Alam?'

'I went for a really lovely meal with a mysterious
sheikh last night. We had such a laugh about all the
players I've worked with and do you know, he taped
it all to listen to when he got home . . .'

UNLIKELY VIDEO GAMES

JUST WANK 2014

NEED FOR SPEED: MOST ADDICTED

CORPSE PARTY: HOUSE OF LORDS

MORTAL WOMBAT

*FIST OF THE LONDON MAYORAL CANDIDATE:
KEN'S RAGE 2*

*ASSASSIN'S CREED: OPERATION
GRASSY KNOLL 1963*

*CALL OF DUTY: CENTRAL LONDON
TRAFFIC WARDEN*

STATE OF DECAY: ORTHODONTIST 3

GREAT BRITISH BAKE OFF: DOUGHRISER

ASHLEY YOUNG: PRO DIVER

LEGO CITY 2, RESIDENT EVIL 2
(after extra time, Lego City won on penalties)

SONIC THE ROADKILL

BAD TITLES FOR MEMOIRS

Baking Bad – *The Nigella Lawson Story*

Gove Actually – *The Secret Life of the Former Secretary of State for Education*

Brake Fast at Tiffany's – *Stopping Suddenly Outside the Homes of Eighties Teen Pop Icons*

Really F**king Bored of Ecuadorian Diplomat Small Talk – *A Year in the Life of Julian Assange*

Airline Revolution: Michael O'Leary and Ryanair (NB: Price £1.99 if you buy online, otherwise £18 bookshop supplement)

Booky F**ky 3 – *Even More Sixth-Form Politics Bollocks* by Russell Brand

The Unauthorized Vladimir Putin by Very, Very, Very Anonymous

Job Done, Feet Up, F**k Off by Andy Murray

Angela Merkel: The Complete Phone Conversations by the NSA

My Greatest Games by Tom Cleverley

Only Fools and Horses – *The Sexual Partners of Princess Anne*

Not Just a Pretty Face – *The Marion Bartoli Story* by John Inverdale

I Am Legend by John Legend

Everything Is Illuminated – *A History of the Osram Light Bulb Company*

Actually, My Teammates Did All the Work by Kevin Pietersen

Am I Still Alive? by Don Estelle from *It Ain't Half Hot Mum*

Explaining Oneself – *A Simple Guide to 'Plebgate' for Proles and Oiks* by Andrew Mitchell, MP

The Female Eunuch by Doreen Eunuch (Mrs)

Malcolm in the Middle – *Cricketing Memories from Former England Fast Bowler Devon Malcolm*

Charlotte's Web – *My Favourite Internet Sites* by Charlotte Church

Secretly, I'm an Absolute Bastard – *The Real Dalai Lama*

UNLIKELY SEXTING

'I loved the picture of your cock. It is the perfect size for me. I am two feet tall.'

'Texting you is making me sooo wet . . . you know how sweaty I get when I have to do anything.'

'Hay babe! I am so into you. I just love how we are on the same levell interlectualy.'

'I am sitting at my desk, texting you and watching porn. Yours sincerely, The Chairman of the British Board of Film Censors.'

'What would you do if I said I was making out with a girl and thinking of what you would do if you were watching us in the bedroom? Let me know. Your husband, Alan.'

'I have just got out of the shower but still feel really dirty . . . I think there must be something wrong with the drains. It stinks, and the water was all brown.'

'Are you ready for dinner – or would you like . . . *dessert* first?'
'No, of course not. Always dessert after the main course. What's wrong with you, woman?'

'Do me like you've never done it before . . . oh . . . you haven't done it before? OK, right.'

'I just saw something hot that made me think of you . . . it was a pig roasting on a spit.'

'I want you now, hun . . . sorry, I promised I wouldn't call you that any more . . . Klaus.'

'I'm naked. Guess what I'm doing . . . nope. I'm having a sh*t. I had to take all my clothes off, as I knew it would be messy.'

'Bring the pole. I will dance for you.'
'Really? Well, that's very kind, but I'm not sure Bogdan is free tonight.'

'On my way to your house. Not wearing any underwear. Just been arrested for indecent exposure.'

'I could only be more into you if I was in you . . . hang on, does that make sense? Have I got that the wrong way round?'

'I have never had sex with anyone as amazing as you – or, indeed, anyone apart from you.'

'If you were with me now, my hands would be very busy . . . fighting you off and making a citizen's arrest.'

'You have no idea how you make me feel when you give it to me from behind . . . mainly because I can't see you, what with you being behind me and that.'

POOR NICKNAMES FOR FOOTBALL CLUBS

PISTACHIOS

THE SH*TMEN

COMBOVERS

THE SITH

SCUM

EXISTENTIALISTS

SLUGS

ASBOS

THE TOSSERS

THE BLACK AND BLUES

ROASTERS

THE OVERPAID

DIVERS

THE LADYBOYS

BLOOD N' SPUNKS

PISSFLAPPERS

UNLIKELY ADVICE FOR
YOUNG FOOTBALLERS

The first touch is vital. If you inform the authorities at this stage, your coach can be prosecuted before things go any further.

Fullbacks: form a successful partnership with your wingman. He starts the conversation, you lead the girl onto the dance floor and then back to your hotel.

It is hugely important to rest and recuperate fully, though ideally not when your opponents are breaking away with the ball.

It's great to warm up with a ball manipulation exercise. I usually continue until I'm fully erect.

Physical and verbal abuse should be eradicated from the game at the very lowest level. And if the little sh*ts don't get the message, give them a slap and a kick up the arse.

Work on your ability in the air: that way, when you dive, you can come down without injury but make it look like you're about to die.

If you're looking to score, make sure to hit the sweet spot. I recommend the Long Bar at the Sanderson – always full of fanny.

Many footballers use left-field activities such as yoga, swimming and cycling to help their game. Alternatively, Diego Maradona's success was fuelled by alcohol, prostitutes and performance-enhancing drugs.

Finishing is a precise art. If you're outside the box, I'd go for on her tits.

The aspiring goalkeeper needs to be acrobatic, alert to game situations and adept at reading the flight of the ball. If not, just try to get really, really fat and fill the goal.

As a defender, try to force things into one direction. The best plan is to target Louis, as he is the smallest – then get your teammate to sit on him while you choose the easiest orifice.

Rule one: as much as you can, try and kick that round thing into the big net thingy.

Creating space is an art form. I like to sh*t myself early in the game, to make it as unpleasant as possible for defenders to stay close to me.

Never stop practicing your crosses, as this means you can always sign a contract even if you are too dense to write your own name.

The most important part of attacking play is working out your goal celebration. You cannot spend enough time on it. When advancing on goal, always work out your dance moves in your head before concentrating on beating the keeper.

Always aim for where the keeper isn't. No, that doesn't mean the crowd, you idiot.

When your team has the ball, everyone is an attacker. When the opposition has the ball, everyone is a defender – unless you're a really famous striker. Then you can ignore the second bit.

Win, lose or draw, if you have given 100 per cent, you are a hero and have nothing to be ashamed of. You might just be sh*te.

Watch Luis Suarez closely to see how he does things: aim for the fleshy part of the inner arm just below the wrist, and nip enough to cause pain without leaving tooth marks.

For goalkeepers, timing when to come out is always difficult. I recommend waiting until you retire and have an autobiography to sell.

BAD TAGLINES FOR MOVIES

The Hobbit: An Unexpected Journey – . . . out of
the cinema, about halfway through the film

What Women Want – Mel Gibson discovers that
it isn't an angry old anti-Semite obsessed with Jesus

The Day After Tomorrow – is when I'll get round to
watching this bollocks

Blue is the Warmest Colour – Look, we know
it's French, but trust us, stick with it. There's some
cracking shagging stuff

The Pianist – Difficult to ask for tickets without
saying 'penis'

Avatar – The dullest 'blue' movie ever

Crash – The Richard Hammond story

Her – You know, that one out of that thing . . .

Mamma Mia – For the ladies and the gays

The Last King of Scotland – The Alex Salmond story

UNLIKELY NAMES FOR RACEHORSES

KICK IN DICK

CYRIL SMITH'S BIG FAT WOBBLY ARSE

I WILL BE GLUE

WRONG HOLE WEDNESDAY

YOUREALLC**TS

BUY MY JIZZ

SURPRISINGLY TASTY

FONDLED BY STABLE BOY

DIDGERIDON'T

ANAL PROLAPSE

UNLIKELY THINGS TO HEAR
AT THE WINTER OLYMPICS

'We've seen Britain on the bobsleigh and the skeleton bob, and now here comes our biggest hope: two chavs on a black bin bag.'

'The British skier has been disqualified – he's tested positive for scarf and mittens.'

'And that's a spin, triple axel, double toe loop, and double somersault! Those hotel steps really should have been cleared of snow.'

'And now, the closest thing to an actual Wacky Races vehicle you will ever see – it's the four-man bobsleigh.'

'Sadly the ice hockey has been rather spoiled by the under-pitch heating.'

'The winning ski-jumper is offering his thank yous to what made it all possible – gravity, mostly.'

'And this is one of those occasions that only occur once every four years – where the British public get to say, "So that's what Robin Cousins looks like nowadays".'

'And there's Britain's Heather Mills in the ice dancing. A fantastic axel spin there, but sadly her leg has flown off and decapitated the Russian judge.'

'The British team are not here yet – their train was delayed by the snow.'

'Hmm. Ironically, the Olympic flame has melted all the snow.'

'And I'm just hearing – yes, it's Gold for the British skier – no, sorry, it's cold for the British skier.'

'Apart from hosting the Olympics, Sochi is of course famous for absolutely nothing.'

'The skiing is cancelled – it's the wrong kind of snow.'

'I'm really not sure those kids should be throwing snowballs at the shooting team.'

'And that's the 87th consecutive figure of eight he's – oh no, he's gone through the ice.'

'And it's gold for the French in the slalom, so they'll enjoy their après-ski – or whatever they call it in France.'

'Everyone's ready for the off – except the British competitors, who have stayed in their hotel rooms moaning about the snow.'

'You join us here at the Winter Olympics, where it's minus 30. And with that kind of score, the British aren't going to win.'

'And after that sudden thaw, it's time for the slush hockey.'

'And for our demonstration sport, a man will try unsuccessfully to rescue his dog from an icy pond.'

'He's that rarest of figure skaters – he's married to a woman.'

UNLIKELY ADVICE FOR
YOUNG FOOTBALLERS

Be careful with your goal celebrations! Rule of thumb: keep your cocks in. Kissing is OK, tugging each other off is a bit much.

The more illiterate and unintelligent you are, the better the footballer you will be. The brain only has so much space, so save it for the beautiful game.

Nicknames: you have to have one. Don't feel like you can only add a 'y' on to your surname. Try adding 'o' or 'sy'. For foreign players, derogatory references to ethnicity are a given; for anyone else, 'Fatso' or 'Wanker' should suffice.

Don't sell yourself short. You have earned the right to shag any woman you like.

Whatever your position, you will have to be able to receive, shoot, pass, dribble and make space – although if you can't do most of the above, you can probably still get 50 caps for England.

The referee's word is final. You have to accept his decision – but feel free to give him the occasional 'accidental' kick in the shins, or volley the ball into his 'nads.

If you have to piss on the pitch, always do it during the opposition anthem, not your own. You'd hate for it to be misinterpreted.

If you are chosen as man of the match, always look as unimpressed as possible with the champagne you are awarded.

Don't waste your playing years worrying about what you'll do when you retire. Either you'll be a manager, a fat pub landlord or you'll be bankrupt, imprisoned and prematurely dead.

Charity work is for pussies.

The national anthem is important. Always sing it, even if the game has kicked off. This may disconcert your opponents, who will think you are mad.

If the crowd is booing you during a game, why not win them over by mocking their appearance, ethnicity, disabilities or ideally, pointing out the huge disparity between your wages and theirs?

Once a week, call a team meeting. This is a great opportunity to point out other players' failings and slag off the manager.

Always take your manager's criticism on board.
Listen intently before nodding and shouting,
'F**k off, you fat c**t. What have you ever won?'
If they're foreign, a simple 'blah, blah, blah, I can't
understand a word' should suffice.

Assert your personality in the dressing room by
trying to shag all of your colleagues' wives. Consider
making up a chart of conquests with photos to see
how the team bonds.

Always keep things in perspective: it isn't about
winning, it's the expensive cars and the glamour
models.

If someone fouls you, punch them repeatedly in the
face. OK, you might get sent off, but it puts down a
marker. Football is all about the bigger picture.

If you want to smoke, smoke.

Anyone who tells you success is all about knuckling
down and working hard is clearly an idiot.
Ignore them.

Parents: Never shout negative comments at your
children from the touchline. Instead, make up
a derogatory song or chant and get everyone to
join in. They have to learn.

AN UNLIKELY GUIDE TO CAMPING

Campsites come in all shapes and sizes, but rest assured, whatever you choose, you're guaranteed a sh*t time.

These days most campsites have toilets, showers and extensive dogging facilities.

To avoid difficulties on arrival, why not try getting it up in your garden before you set off? At least you'll have some pleasure before the awful camping business starts.

Always pack your tent last in the car. There's then a very good chance you'll forget it, and you can all book into a Premier Inn or something.

Poles should be fed carefully through the flysheet. Don't ask me why; these people just come over here with their funny Eastern European ways.

Always aim to be near a source of clean water . . . like a hotel, or your house.

If you are feeling cold and not enjoying your night, bring your still-warm barbecue into the tent with you. Soon, your worries will be over.

Rules to Remember: Leave No Trace! Ensure the grave is at least six feet . . . oh, sorry, I mean tidy up after yourself.

Remember not to sh*t in your tent. It can make for a long, unpleasant night's sleep.

UNLIKELY LINES FROM A SEX MANUAL

That's frankly disgusting.

Much pleasure can be gained from placing it on the table and smashing it repeatedly with a hammer.

Nutcrackers are an often overlooked staple of sexual foreplay.

Do not try to replicate the position in Diagram 4. It's a misprint.

Join the dots to create a really massive cock and balls.

Never, ever do this.

Which one of these is not a vagina?

If your penis is smaller than the one in the diagram . . . forget it.

Wahey!

If she screams and runs away, check you did Part One properly.

If semen is pulsing out by the ladleful, call a doctor.

The more you use the word 'jizz', the more romantic the evening.

Chapter 5: Things That Are Illegal but Fun

Chapter 6: Things That Are Illegal and Hurt

Chapter 7: Shoving Stuff Up Arses

Try to avoid saying 'yeah, baby, harder, harder' if you don't want to sound like a twat.

*One technique I advise is to keep repeating 'f**k, f**k, f**k' until she just leaves.*

Rubbing that vigorously is good; rubbing this vigorously is a no-no.

Be safe and sexy by checking each other for lumps and bumps (smear tests and colonoscopies are probably overdoing it).

Play 'dirty dice'. Roll a number and equate it to a dirty deed – then pay your girlfriend £200, and go straight to jail.

AN UNLIKELY GUIDE TO
KEEPING TROPICAL FISH

NEVER take a fish to a football match, as the singing and chanting makes them nervous.

As fish get bigger, they will want to sit next to you in the front seat. Just say no. It is much safer in the back.

Timeless rule no. 1: If it's green, kill it.

*Timeless rule no. 2: If it has spots, don't f**k it.*

Timeless rule no. 3: If anyone can see you doing it, stop immediately.

You can't reason with a baby fish. You must use discipline. Remember, you are its owner, not its friend.

Most fish will outlive you, so prepare thoroughly for a time when you will no longer be there (however, don't discuss these arrangements in front of your fish, it will only upset them).

Start each day by walking naked up to the tank and screaming 'Hello, fish!' until you pass out.

I have mixed feelings about small, brightly coloured fish because my brother was mugged by one.

When push comes to shove, most fish are wankers.

Sharks make tricky pets. It's worth it if you persevere, but don't try unless you have a longish bath.

I think it's fair to say that everybody has a funny fish anecdote.

Fish are more intelligent than humans, so watch out. You need to be on guard 24/7.

Tropical fish sex may be brief, but they are, in general, gentle and grateful lovers.

To keep tropical fish as a hobby, you need two things: money, and a total absence of anything else happening in your life.

Tropical fish are notoriously private, so chances to watch them have sex are few and far between.

If you find your fish floating upside down in the water, it's probably the work of Mossad.

Those little lines of matter hanging down from a fish are not its waste products, but its discarded hopes and dreams.

Try not to fish in front of young fish . . . it upsets them.

One rule of thumb: if it's over 30 feet, for God's sake get it out of the house!

Strangely, they still count as tropical even if you bought them from a bloke with a van full of tanks in Widnes.

BAD NAMES FOR NEW BOYBANDS

F**K THAT

TIME OF THE MONTH

IBS

RIPPER STREET

HEALTH & EFFICIENCY

HATTERSLEY

ANAL

CLOSET

READER'S DIGEST

MUTANT GENE

GET IN LANE

MENGELE

GASH

BUKKAKE

NCP

ISLAMIC JIHAD

TIFFIN

THE FINGERING

COLLYMORE

BALLSACK

JIM'LL FIX IT

UNLIKELY ADVICE FOR MOUNTAINEERS

Remember: climbing a mountain is hard.
Falling off one is a piece of piss.

Before climbing, assess your mental strength.
Are you positive and a good problem solver, or are
you thinking, 'Arrgghhh, look at the size of that
f**ker! We're all going to die!'?

No mountain should be climbed alone. Try and
make sure you are accompanied by at least one
experienced mountaineer or, failing that, someone
really fat who will make for a soft landing.

Crampons are easy to use. Just relax, and gently
insert into the body cavity . . . oh, sorry, you said
crampons.

When choosing your ice axe, check the length,
grip the head and tweak the leash . . . ooh, sorry,
I've come.

Stay with the other climbers at all times, even if
they are having a sh*t behind a bush.

Aim low for your first climbs. Try a challenging but ultimately achievable ascent, such as going up Primrose Hill when it's a bit wet.

When tackling your first mountain, check out what service huts are available at base camp. Don't expect a Pizza Express or a Starbucks! (NB: there'll probably be a Subway and a fried-chicken outlet, though.)

When approaching the top of a glacier, always be careful in case there is a polar bear standing on top of it.

Hold your ice axe by the head with your uphill hand. Place your thumb under the adze and your palm and forefingers around the pick, raise above your shoulder and plunge by throwing your weight. This should give you enough ice for a few G&Ts while the other losers climb the mountain.

UNLIKELY ADVICE FOR GOLFERS

Hit that little white thing with one of these sticks in the bag. Try not to let it fall down that hole thing.

One method that works for me is to visualize the ball running on to the green. I see the green as an arse and the hole as an anus with the ball being a small, round, white cock . . . I've said too much, haven't I?

One good way to win is to kick your opponent's ball into the lake.

An important tip when you are getting started is to buy the ugliest trousers you can find and become a bore.

An albatross is annoying, but bogeys are much more common and should be wiped away immediately.

Grab the shaft, hold it tightly with both hands, swing both ways, raise it above your head, bring it down fast and then follow it round behind your back. Now, put it away and pick up your golf club.

If you find yourself in the rough during a game, try and finish off as quickly as you can, send her on her way as chivalrously as possible and then continue with the round.

One good thing about golf is . . . err . . . ah, right, where were we?

If you've hit the water, try and swim to shore. In this scenario, survival and searching for other passengers must take precedence over playing golf.

After a while you will learn to distinguish between a sand wedge and a sandwich, which will surely cut down on your orthodontist bills.

One good way to improve your game and gain respect is to shout 'c**t!' every time you make a mistake.

The great thing about golf is that it doesn't take up much time or money, so it fits well into a busy schedule.

Try to avoid smacking the ball straight into the face of an annoying spectator.

Before hitting the ball, check it is not an explosive.

Although it is not encouraged, it is not prohibited to pick up the ball and drop it in the hole if you get fed up.

Try to avoid starting your round by shouting 'Hello, wankers' to everyone you meet.

Good ways to distract your opponent during their swing are to pretend to sneeze, fart or go 'Boing!'

If your ball lands in excrement, change your underwear.

If you hit a ball and hook it by accident towards any bystanders, you can shout 'Fore!', or – more fun, in my opinion – do nothing, and let nature take its course.

BAD THINGS TO SAY AT CUSTOMS

'I have nothing to declare . . . except this massive boner.'

'No, hang on, heroin is legal in my country.'

'Have you got a match? My shoes have gone out.'

'OK. I admit it, I've hidden it in one of my bodily cavities. See if you can find it . . . starting now.'

'Proceed up your red channel? My, you are forward in this country!'

'Yes, it is crack cocaine, but it's for purely medical purposes.'

'Business or pleasure? Well, both. I'm a rent boy.'

'Can I just declare I am absolutely sweating cobs? Is it bloody boiling in here or is it me?'

'Actually, it doesn't matter, I've drunk the 22 litres of beer while I was queuing to come through this gate.'

'Yes, ma'am, I am concealing a weapon, but it only ever exceeds 50cm in length if I'm really pleased to see you.'

UNLIKELY GUIDE FOR MOTORCYLISTS

If your passenger has suddenly gone quiet, it might be time to pull over.

Chapter 32: Motorways, and How to Shoot a Rival Hell's Angel while Travelling on One

Motorbikes sound like this, don't they? Vroom, vroom, vroom, vroom, *nerr nerr nerr nerr*, brrruuummmmm . . . (cont. pp 34–123)

Of course, if it's raining, then you can't go out.

Traffic lights, lane markers, roundabouts: these don't apply to you. Skip to the next chapter.

When setting off with a sidecar attached, always ensure you are aware you are no longer living in 1957.

Chapter 2: HELMET. Right: enough of the insults, let's get back to the bike.

Remember: you will almost certainly die.

If you want to know where reverse is, you are almost certainly too stupid to be allowed near a motorbike.

Chapter 3: Growing Your Goatee, Getting Your Tattoo and Earring, Handling Your Divorce

If you can't close your legs easily, then you might have a problem. Anyway, now back to the motorbike.

Remember: sticking your cock in an exhaust pipe is painful. Don't do it.

UNLIKELY VIDEO GAMES

LEGO GRAND THEFT AUTO

KNITMASTER VS W.I.

'MANHUNT' FROM GRINDR

PAINKILLER: HEADACHE AND FEVER

TIGER WOODS: PRO SHAGGER 2014

JUST TWERK WITH ERIC PICKLES

CRAZY MINICAB

*THE SIMS 10: SMALL ESTATE
OF 3- AND 4-BEDROOMED HOUSES
OUTSIDE NUNEATON*

MEP – LATE NIGHT SITTING 2: STRASBOURG

WEATHER FORECASTER 3

CRASH BANDICOOT: TODDLER ATTACK

AL-ZAWAHIRI'S JIHADI WARRIOR 2

*SUPER MARIO BROTHERS: LATE NIGHT
DRAINAGE EMERGENCY 4*

*THE WANKING DEAD, EPISODE 8:
THE CRUSTY SOCK*

LEGO CITY: CRACK DEN

BAD THINGS FOR A NEW ENGLAND FOOTBALL MANAGER TO SAY

'Well, I'm not choosing any f**king Liverpool players.
Red Sh*te.'

'As the Son of God . . .'

'I want to be the first manager to win the World Cup
for England . . . hmm? What? Really? I had no idea.'

'Look, I may be a proud Scotsman, but I've every
intention of working with these arrogant pricks
to bring out the very best in their cheating,
one-dimensional game plan.'

'I'm more of a rugger man, really, chaps.'

'We have a good record against Germany.
Not in football, admittedly, but in warfare we're
all over them.'

'Ooh, it's raining. Quick, pass me that umbrella.'

'How long till half time? I'm bursting for a sh*t.'

UNLIKELY NAMES FOR RACEHORSES

WASH YOUR BALLS

GRIEVOUS BODILY HARM

CARDINAL WOLSEY

DISHONOURABLE DISCHARGE

ABBATOIR

ENFORCED PRISON HOMOSEXUALITY

SPECTACLES, TESTICLES, WALLET & PHONE

CAR PARK FLASHER

RUNNING SH*T

GUN TO THE HEAD

UNLIKELY SCENES FROM A CHICK-LIT NOVEL

What if he isn't the one? What if it wasn't meant to be? Oh, who cares? This is all bollocks.

The Wednesday fans were throwing bricks onto us in the bus station, so we got tooled up with iron bars and blades and went steaming in to 'em. 'F**k you. The Firm are in town.'

Weight 19st 4, alcohol units 48, cigarettes 102, calories 8,000. Hmm! Had a bit of a blowout yesterday, dear diary.

I tightened the rope round his neck and just pulled it tighter and tighter until his face reddened, his eyes bulged and he breathed no more.

'Why are you so certain he's Mr Wrong?' I shouted.
'No, Mr Wong!' Clara shouted back. 'He's Chinese!'

After we did eventually get together, it turns out we didn't have that much in common, and it just sort of fizzled out. THE END

If I'd waited for the next bus as I had planned to, I would never have gone up to the top deck, caught him wanking on the back seat and broken the ice with the man of my dreams.

She was a shopaholic. What was that about? Well, it was a by-product of her serious mental health issues and an expression of the pain she still felt after a brutal, alienating childhood at the hands of parents with drink problems.

So in the end, I just gave him a blow job and that was that.

TIPS ON WORKPLACE ETIQUETTE

Try to do as little as possible whilst looking as busy as possible. Never do the reverse, as it makes us all look bad.

If your boss tells a joke, laugh – for hours if necessary. If someone subordinate to you tells a joke, tell them to shut the f**k up and smash their head on the desk. They need to learn.

If someone brings a dog to work, no one is going to give you a hard time if you decide to kill it. Make it quick and humane. However, Bring a Child to Work Day is different.

Chewing your pencil is OK. Chewing your boss is not.

Chapter 27: What to Do If You Find a Witch

Chapter 29: The Office and Faeces

Chapter 33: Why You Must Never Treat Women as Equals

Chapters 50–55: Where to Hide Cheese in an Office

Chapter 60: Buttocks and Photocopiers

Chapter 61: Cocks and Ink Wells

Chapter 62: Testicles and Tea Cups

Chapters 71–83: Practical Jokes and When to Stop[†] ([†]Never)

Chapter 83: Rimming and Fingering

UNLIKELY LINES FROM A SEX MANUAL

*If you are going 'down under', make sure you know
who she is.*

*Sometimes the feeling of pleasure can be enhanced
by scents, low lighting, mood music and the
inclusion of her mother.*

*If you must fart when receiving oral pleasure,
make sure it is definitely only a fart.*

Chapter 45: Disposing of Witnesses

Chapter 50: What to Do If You Get Stuck in a Hole

*If a stream of white stuff comes out of the end, you are
a witch who must be burned at the stake.*

*Using pet names can enhance intimacy.
Try 'Fido', 'Spot', 'Rover', 'Shep' or 'Gnasher'.*

*Break the ice by browsing sexy websites, flicking
through erotic magazines, or popping the ice you've
broken into a drink laced with Rohypnol.*

*Set aside thirty minutes every Sunday to relax with
each other and discuss your fantasies. This will give
you time to chat, have sex three times and then
do the housework – or is this just me?*

*Women: a man is aroused through his skin. Take time
to learn the art of erotic touch, light candles, oil up your
hands and his skin, and then gently explore his tender
nakedness . . . Oh, all right, the best thing to do is
wank him off.*

Sex things up by always sleeping in the nude (unless you're on a night flight, or are dozing off on the bus).

Keep sex alive by changing your routine and having sex at different times of the day, in different places . . . f*ck it, just have an affair with someone else.

Sex in forbidden places can be a huge turn-on. Maybe try it in your parents' bed. In most cases, this is better attempted when they are out.

Wear wigs to bed to excite your boyfriend by pretending you are someone else. You may want to draw the line at a moustache and strap-on.

Why not surprise your husband by occasionally removing your pubic hair completely? Or, for an even bigger surprise, try removing his in one fell swoop without warning him.

Have sex in water – though if you're doing oral, best make it fast.

BAD ADVICE FOR MEDICAL SELF-DIAGNOSIS

Any spot or mole on your body is almost certainly cancer. If you find a spot or mole, drive to the nearest hospital, dash through the gates and run to the desk screaming, 'I've got cancer! I've got cancer!' This way, people will know what you're talking about and will take you seriously.

Is there any rough skin around the vagina? Steady, guys . . . this is for girls only.

What colour is your stool? Does it smell? Have you had it varnished and placed it at the breakfast bar? If yes, you need to abandon this weird behaviour and flush it down the toilet.

Never wash your hands – it takes you further from God.

When talking to a receptionist, don't say balls, say testicles; don't say sh*t, say faeces; don't say brown, say Hovis.

One sign that things may be going wrong is if it falls off. If it does fall off, stand still and whimper.

Does your penis look anything like the diagrams in this book? If yes, then you're weird, because these are diagrams of noses.

Are your breasts lump-free and smooth? Check them yourself. Now, let me, can I touch them? Can I? Can I? You said I could if I bought you that handbag! You promised!

A rectal thermometer should be disposed of after one use. Don't even think of giving it as a present.

POOR NICKNAMES FOR FOOTBALL CLUBS

DODOS

THE WEEDS

GOD BOTHERERS

BIG FAT GYPSIES

THE BLUE TITS

SMACKHEADS

MASS MURDERERS

THE FADGE

YOUNG GIRLS

LUFTWAFFE

NOT VERY GOODIES

THE ADDICTS

MOOMINS

KHMER ROUGE

JOBBIES

SCRUBBERS

UNLIKELY LINES FROM A BRITISH GANGSTER FILM

'Torch his car? As in set it on fire? Isn't that illegal?'

'I get my money by noon on Tuesday, or I'll draw a cock and balls on your car.'

'Methinks wit is more necessary than beauty, and I think no young woman ugly that has it, and no handsome woman agreeable without it.'

'I'm not scared of him, Boss – he's just a journeyman footballer who can't act.'

'He's a big man, but he's out of shape . . . so he shouldn't be wearing those trousers with that top.'

'Oh, what a beautiful morning! Oh, what a wonderful day! Come on, everybody . . .'

'No, let's leave it, Smasher, it's raining.'

'To be honest, your terms seem a bit excessive, so I'd quite like to shop around for protection online.'

'Pete, keep tickling him until he talks.'

'OK, I've had enough of your excuses, John – write that he loves cock as his Facebook status.'

'That Jack "the Hat" McVitie really takes the biscuit.'

'I'm not your friend anymore, you big fat poo-poo.'

UNLIKELY THINGS TO HEAR
ON DAYTIME TV

'These four date from the early part of the century, some tarnishing and wear: please welcome today's *Loose Women*.'

'I'm afraid there's been a murder. Somebody got sick to death of Angela Lansbury being on every day, and shot her.'

'The next programme is Pointless . . . yes, it's the Jeremy Kyle show.'

'Now for some more programmes that will make you think twice about taking a day off sick again.'

'Here's today's *Countdown* conundrum: why is *Countdown* still on?'

'That's it for today. We hope you'll still be unemployed tomorrow, and will join us again.'

'After presenting 200 of these tedious property shows, I can now afford to swap my inner-city flat for a large house in the country.'

'After all that, the Wilsons decided not to buy a house in the sun. But they did thank us for a lovely free holiday in Spain.'

'Up next, Billy the Kid constructs a bungalow with Wild Bill Hickok in this week's *Cowboy Builders*.'

BAD THINGS TO ADMIT

'Well, the thing with Operation Yewtree is, there but for the grace of God . . .'

'Well, yes that bit is a lie. But everyone lies on their CV, don't they?'

'Yes. I have been to a Harvester before.'

'I'm Lord Lucan.'

'I'm a massive fan of the comedian Dieudonné.'

'I'll always remember where I was when I heard the news about Diana's death. I was having my white Fiat Uno repaired in a garage outside Paris after a minor collision the night before.'

'Yes. Not only did I spill your pint, but I was also looking at you in a funny way.'

'No, I haven't heard the good news about Jesus. Tell me more.'

'That smell? I've just farted.'

'I always cry at the end of *Bambi* . . . or, in fact, any time I've been masturbating.'

'What am I thinking? That you're a massive c**t.'

'No, I didn't pack this bag myself. I left it to my friends Abu Jihadi and Carlos "The Colombian Devil" Escobar.'

'No, it was 2008 when you went on that beach holiday in Greece. I know from all the times I've been through your Facebook photo albums while wanking.'

'My heroes? Nick Clegg first, then Nick Knowles second.'

'Hobbies? Errm . . . eating out, keeping fit, watching movies and killing drifters.'

'I'm not that pleased to see you, but I do currently have an erection, since you mention it.'

'I thought *you* were checking the parachutes.'

'Yes, I can spare a minute to talk to you about famine in the Third World.'

'This is my first date for a while. I usually just stay in, wrap myself in cling film and watch porn on my laptop.'

'I was surprised too when the temping agency offered me this job as a heart surgeon. But it seems like we've gotten away with it, eh?'

UNLIKELY THINGS TO READ
IN A TRAVEL GUIDE

One foolproof and fun way to catch hepatitis is . . .

But the main thing to bear in mind as you walk the streets abroad is that foreigners are twats.

*The phrase 'you fat ugly c**t' is useful, if used in moderation.*

The climate here can vary enormously between very hot during the day and very cold during the night, so, to be honest, I wouldn't bother going.

The gallery has some of the finest and best-preserved works of art in the world. But if it's hookers you're looking for, I suggest the old Asian quarter.

It's a long, steep climb, but it really is worth it. Particularly if your partner is fat and at risk of a heart attack.

Here in the old docks there are fascinating old schooners and a wonderful maritime museum. But more importantly, there are rough old sailors prepared to stick it up you for 50 Kr.

The culture is great in Germany, but the food is not, so I suggest bringing all your own food for the two weeks in your rucksack.

For a really fun, exciting night of local culture, I recommend a stoning at the local football stadium.

UNLIKELY CHEESE NAMES

SPANISH DONKEY CHEESE

MOGADISHU

MILD RACIST

SEPP BLATTER

ROYAL MURDER

CROYDON BLUE

SHILTON

RANCID COCK

SOLZHENITSYN

REEKING FRENCHIE

UNLIKELY THINGS TO HEAR IN
A WEATHER FORECAST

'Let's get a report on the strength of that hurricane in Oklahoma – our reporter is now in Texas.'

'That's unbelievable: it actually is raining men.'

'So that's 2 degrees – and I can still only get a job as a weathergirl on local radio.'

'No need for coats today, in fact it's T-shirt weather – so that's minus 5 degrees, here in Newcastle.'

'On this typically British June day, we've had four seasons in a day: winter, winter, autumn and winter.'

'I'm afraid our long-term forecasting system is down at the moment – I left my piece of seaweed at home.'

'In the early hours tonight, I'm afraid there'll be the possibility of widespread damp patches in southern parts, as I'm getting drunk and will probably wet the bed.'

'I've had a letter from a viewer asking how I can say with any certainty that there'll be a 50 per cent chance of rain. Well, that's what happens when you toss a coin.'

UNLIKELY THINGS TO READ IN A PORN MAG

'Stop!' he said. 'How do I know this is what we both want? Let's talk about where this is going.'

TALK to Filthy Female Students Now! Warn them not to squander their opportunities, to beware of fungal infections and of over-borrowing on student loans.

She watched intently as he removed his clothes and stood proudly in the shimmering moonlight. Turned out his penis was average at best, and he was quite fat and spotty.

TITS! ARSE! BLOW JOBS! Now I've got your attention: have you ever considered a career in the IT industry?

Slowly, the plumber reached into his trousers and pulled out his truly enormous rod. Clearly, the blockage in the drain was going to be quite difficult to dislodge.

FREE in this month's issue of *Celebrity Skin*: a bit of Mick Hucknall's psoriasis.

READER'S LETTERS: Dear '*Barely Legal Fat Muffs, incorp. Gerbil Inserter*': I am worried that my husband might be having an affair. What do you suggest I do?

THIS MONTH! Hunky Eric Pickles and Ken Clarke show us their 'red boxes' in pictures that are anything but Conservative!

Welcome to *9 Inches*! We're banned in Europe – not for our content, but because of the metric system!

Welcome to ALL NEW 'Reader's Dogs' – for seriously sick puppies!

BAD THINGS TO SAY AT CUSTOMS

'Are these children mine? Well, yes . . . I guess they are now.'

'I am transporting two adult male gerbils into this country. Unfortunately they are currently quite a long way up my arse.'

'Business or pleasure? Well, I suppose you'd have to say that in a way, jihad is both.'

'Oh, no. Are you guys going to deny me entry agaaaaaiiiin?'

'Yo! Wassup, dickhead?'

'I want to request a woman to look through my luggage. I know I'm a man, but I just want to see her pick up the illegal sex toys.'

'How dare you, Officer! Just because we don't have the same surname doesn't mean he isn't my son! Granted, the fact he's a different colour, is begging for help and is two years older than me are a different matter.'

'Business or pleasure? Ha! What do you think? Have you seen this bloody country?'

'I assure you this is not from Cuba, sir. They don't have ivory in Cuba!'

'I am not travelling alone. It's me, the ghost of my dear wronged father, and my invisible cat, Horace. Say hello.'

BAD THINGS TO HEAR ON
A SPACE STATION

'What's that twitching under your rib cage, Johnson?'

'So I started with some Bowie; and now I'm going to sing you some James Blunt.'

'OK, you two. Turns out I *can* hear you scream.'

'Toilet's blocked.'

'Hello. This is Ground Control. Hope you're all OK? Um . . . have you all made wills?'

'Well, the bad news is, we've lost Kowalski into deep space . . . the good news is, I probably don't need to bother watching *Gravity*.'

'Right. Come on. Back out on the moon for another nine holes.'

'Sh*t! I think I left the gas on at home!'

'Eh? What do you mean, the neighbours have come to complain about the noise?'

'Bloody hell. I've just checked my bill online, and these roaming charges are killing me.'

UNLIKELY THINGS TO READ IN A DIET BOOK

Here's a new twist on the 5:2 Diet – if you eat five meals a day, try only eating two.

Eat as much as you want, and still lose weight – simply lick a toilet seat and get dysentery.

And if it all goes wrong, you can stand on this book and get the biscuit tin off the top shelf.

An apple a day keeps the doctor away – as do new pricing structures for GP out-of-hours care.

Are you overweight because of an overactive thyroid and big bones? Well, stop eating those kebabs.

The diet book to help and encourage all types of big fat fatty-fat fats.

Remember, there are good fats and bad fats. You, you're one of the bad fats.

The big problem is trans fats: transsexual fat people.

Putting a picture of yourself naked on the fridge door can work wonders, although it did get me the sack from work.

THINGS A SPORTS COMMENTATOR
WOULD NEVER SAY

'He's got four from just the one ball: what a lot of children
Lance Armstrong has fathered.'

'The fans are all shouting, "In the hole, in the hole".
An outrageous way to behave at someone's funeral.'

'Let's see if we can find a hotspot on the replay . . . mmm –
looks like someone had a curry last night.'

'You're watching in widescreen, HD, 3D Nicam stereo – but
ultimately I'm afraid it's still golf.'

'Rooney, turns, dribbles, swivels, pauses quickly to pick up a
bit of brain that's fallen out of his head, and shoots.'

'Scotland have scored again, and they're into double figures.
That's 11 runs they have. So, with Scotland 11 for 7 against
the Long Crendon Village XI, it's back to you in the studio.'

'As they come to the chequered flag – hooray! Another crash!
Look, he's on fire. Brilliant.'

'And, as feared, there has been a violent clash in the cricket
between India and Pakistan. Pale blue and bright green
really doesn't work at all.'

UNLIKELY THINGS TO HEAR
IN HOSPITAL

'Mr Smith, we've removed half your liver and one kidney and replaced them with the cornflakes you asked for.'

'Well, Mrs Jones, to give you an idea of how badly swollen those tonsils are, we're going to have to get a gynaecologist to take them out.'

'Start counting backwards from ten – when you get to one, it's your turn to try and find me.'

'We're collecting for the nurses. Have you got any spare nurses you don't need?'

'The good news is, we've taken your stitches out; the bad news is, your leg fell off.'

'Oops – clumsy me! I meant the *patient's* left, not your left.'

'I've removed twelve inches of bowel, which means I can now accurately measure that gap where I wanted to put some shelves.'

'Start counting backwards from ten million – when you get to one, that's when you can have your operation.'

'While you wait for the consultant to come back with the results, why not have a look at this coffin catalogue?'

UNLIKELY THINGS TO READ
IN A TRAVEL GUIDE

Oh yeah, they were a massive help in the war, weren't they?
F**king collaborators.

The local liquor is strong enough to wake you from the dead,
and it is delicious. I think the best way to enjoy it is to take
a bottle up to the top of the church tower and drink until
you are sick.

*One thing I have learned from bitter experience is that **they***
*are allowed to throw a donkey off a tower, but **you** are not.*

I can never look down at the Champs-Élysées, with its
wonderful line of sight ending at the Eiffel Tower, without
thinking of those wonderful old films of Nazi soldiers and
Hitler's henchmen gathering around it.

The toilets here are frankly a bit dodgy, so try and go before
you get to Heathrow.

I sat there with Sebastien, my flamboyant friend, as we
sipped our espressos, their bitterness offset by the sweetness
of the cool night air. Giddy with the romance of it all,
Seb leapt to his feet, broke into song . . . and was brutally
beaten up by a passing group of drunken England
football fans.

Remember: in France it is an offence to wash on two consecutive days.

One thing the locals absolutely love is when you break into 'Two World Wars and One World Cup'.

Vegetarians are going to find it difficult to eat here, so the best advice is to grow up and stop being so fussy.

In Austria the scenery is quite breathtaking. The locals are a bit less attractive – minging, I'd go so far as to say.

Since the fall of the Berlin Wall, a wonderful neo-Nazi nightlife has sprung up here.

*The once fine buildings are impressive but crumbling now. Well, it's their f**king fault for booting us out. OK, you don't want to be in our empire? OK. Put up your own f**king buildings, then.*

The city is best explored with a guide, but make sure Brown Owl doesn't know you've taken her with you.

UNLIKELY LINES FROM
A SELF-HELP BOOK

Get a grip, you wuss.

If you read this book to the end you will be a success, but
never as successful as me. Just so you know.

When it comes to fulfilling your ambitions, there is a lot
to be learned from slugs.

When people start to believe in themselves, then they start
to become remarkable. They also start to become
really bloody irritating.

Do you think you might be a closet homosexual?

The world is divided into two lots of people:
the Whites and the Others.

How to Stop Worrying and Start Dying

Conquer the World, the Adolf Hitler Way

Just do what I do. Forge a load of certificates from
a made-up university, act confident. No one checks up.
You'll make a fortune at this self-help sh*t.

To drink champagne, you first have to eat sh*t.
And when I say 'eat sh*t', I mean it literally.

REJECTED QUESTIONS FROM
THIS YEAR'S EXAMS

1. If a train leaves Wales at nine o'clock in the morning, how thrilled are the passengers that they don't have to spend another night there?

2. What is the maximum thrust needed to escape the pull of the Earth's gravity? Come on, it's not rocket science.

3. Explain how you would perform a full frontal lobotomy. Come on, it's not brain surgery.

4. Order these stages of a frog's life cycle: tadpole, frogspawn, adult, adult inflated by straw up arse.

5. Religious studies: if two men have been married for ten years, how long will they burn in hell for?

6. Mathematics: please complete the questions in the allotted time. You have eleventy-two minutes.

7. Home Economics: tasting practical. Time's up. Finish the mouthful you're on.

8. With reference to The Merchant of Venice: if Antonio had owed a pound of flesh to Wonga.com instead of to Shylock, how much flesh would he have owed by the end of one week?

9. Are these multiple choice exams too easy? (a) Yes

10. English: write a sentence using the word 'unite' in its new sense of causing division.

11. Spanish: can you translate this phrase into conversational Spanish? 'I want to sell my house for one euro. Where is the soup kitchen?'

12. History: explain the role played by Adolf Hitler and the Nazi party in keeping Channel Five going.

13. Fractions: is Michael Gove too smarmy by (a) half, or (b) two-thirds?

14. Convert 50 per cent into a fraction. This will count as half, or 50 per cent, of your mark.

15. Eton College Maths Paper, Question 1: If Josh spends £10,000 on a crate of Chateau Rothschild and Quentin spends £1,000 on foie gras, how much of their weekly allowance will they have left for coke and prozzies?

16. What chemicals would you typically find hidden in Nigella Lawson's handbag?

17. If it takes four men three days to paint a house of average size, how long will it take a couple of Bulgarians?

18. If my penis spurts out 10cc of sperm in one ejaculation, and my sperm count is normal, how many sperm will have emerged? And also, why isn't my wife pregnant?

19. Using examples from personal history, when does 'no' mean 'no'?

20. If you unwound all of Michael Gove's intestines and laid them in a line, how many teachers would cheer?

21. If Jeremy smells of piss and Johnny smells of poo, shouldn't they stop doing this exam and leave the room?

22. Do you (a) agree, (b) agree strongly, (c) disagree, or (d) disagree strongly?

23. English Literature: What are you f**king staring at, you c**t?

24. If this carrot measures 4cm by 4cm, is it a square root?

25. Suicide Exam: Oh, what's the f**king point?

UNLIKELY THINGS TO READ
IN A ROMANTIC NOVEL

There was something irresistible about Prince Andrew . . .

'I knew you and I would get together, from the moment I took your car keys out of the fruit bowl.'

'That's it – now slip the third finger in. I told you ten-pin bowling would be a fun date.'

After gently undoing her bra he caressed her shoulders, then moved slowly round to her front, where he held his hands over her heaving breasts and went 'Honk, honk!'

'And if I turn out my pockets, and then slide this open here – there you go, your Ladyship – an elephant!'

'Sir, I would like to ask you for your daughter's hand in marriage. Failing that, could she nosh me off behind the conservatory?'

'And now I have put this ring on you, you are officially mine. I know it's not normal for a farmer to marry one of his pigs, but I just don't care.'

'Pray, would you accompany me on a horse ride this morning? The view from the hill is marvellous at this time of year. Plus, I like the way your tits bounce up and down.'

'Will you marry me, make me the happiest man in the world, take my name, and become Mrs Goatybollocks?'

At first glance he knew she was the woman for him. Such beautiful tattoos, and nearly all of them spelled correctly.

UNLIKELY THINGS TO HEAR
ON DAYTIME TV

'Next, *Murder, She Wrote* – where Jessica Fletcher investigates the victim's family, and tries to smear them.'

'As usual, there'll be no episode of *Doctors* this Saturday, as they're refusing to work weekends.'

'You're watching Daytime on ITV – sponsored by Prozac.'

'Next up, another chance to see a classic episode from a vintage series – oh, all right then, it's a repeat.'

'Welcome to The History Channel. It's 6 a.m., and you're watching *Wake Up With Hitler.*'

'Welcome to *Tipping Point*, the show that makes you realize you've wasted another day of your miserable life.'

'And now on BBC Parliament, recorded coverage of the Welsh First Minister's Questions. Why are you watching this? Have you fallen? Do you need an ambulance?'

'Welcome to the weekend episode of *Doctors*, where all the usual cast have been replaced by really poor foreign actors who can barely speak English.'

'In this afternoon's *Murder, She Wrote*, an old woman is murdered for an inheritance. That's followed by *Cash in the Attic.*'

UNLIKELY THINGS TO HEAR
IN A WEATHER FORECAST

'I'm expecting drifts up to six inches deep tonight – I really **must** do something about my dandruff.'

'It's going to be the hottest day of the year so far. That's the forecast for January the first.'

'Let's look at the five-day forecast, which is that large map of the British Isles with the words "No idea" stamped over it.'

'Well, it's sunny tomorrow, so if you're sitting outside having strawberries at Wimbledon, don't forget to put some cream on.'

'And it's good news for ducks – not so much the rain, but I'm having the sesame prawn toast to start.'

'There's a flood warning currently in operation in Cornwall. I think I left the bath running in our holiday cottage.'

'Is it me, or is it, like, really hot?'

'A quick look at the satellite picture – and this one's Sputnik.'

'When we asked you to send in your photos, Mr Jones of Plymouth, those aren't the ones we meant.'

'It will be chilly here, here and here – in this long, thin country next to Argentina.'

UNLIKELY LINES FROM A SEX MANUAL

Chapter 14: Gerbils and Other Rodents

Chapter 22: The Mill on the Floss

If his cock actually crows, be very afraid.

A failsafe is to grab it quickly and keep twisting until your partner faints.

One bad sign is the police arriving.

Chapter 91: Threesomes, and Why My Wife Won't Let Me

Sex can be a joy for almost everyone – but not for you, you big fat pig.

Sometimes a swift poke in the eye is the only thing that will stop him.

Some people think that feet are unattractive and play no part in the sexual act. Others disagree. The latter are insane and should be trusted with nothing.

Cover it with brandy, and light.

Both partners should be equally active in bed. This rule is not applicable if you are a necrophile.

One good method is to practice on a vacuum cleaner or exhaust pipe.

Ejaculation is for procreation only. If you do it more than three or four times in your life, you are doing something wrong.

On a first date, try to avoid leaping onto her shouting 'Yee-ha! Ride 'em, cowboy!'

Whatever you may have read, in my experience, ejaculation will usually be achieved after three or four seconds.

Keep grinding away until one or both of you can't walk.

Anal sex is underrated, especially if you like a bit of poo on the end of your willy.

Never underestimate the sheer joy, and indeed power, of dogging.

Put it in, pull it out, put it in, pull it out . . . and repeat until something happens.

Smells are liberating, within reason.

Attention, men: foreplay is important. Try to set a mood by shouting 'hubba, hubba, hubba' and 'boing, boing, boing' as often as you can.

UNLIKELY THINGS TO READ IN A DIET BOOK

However bad the cravings get, don't eat this book.

Men: how to make the perfect porridge. First, remove your pants . . .

Lose weight instantly: stand on the scales, and then take off that heavy overcoat.

Foreword by Eric Pickles

For drastic weight loss: when you've tried everything else, cut off your arm.

Is being fat ruining your life? Take that cake out of the oven and put your head in there instead.

The 5:2 Diet: restrict yourself to two bags of crisps every five pints.

The cabbage soup diet: not only will you lose weight, but you'll clear the room at dinner parties when you let one go.

Suckling pig, pork bellies . . . if these are some of the names you're called, you really do need this book.

This diet has been used successfully by many royals: Henry VIII, George IV and Queen Victoria.

UNLIKELY THINGS TO HEAR
IN HOSPITAL

'What the hell is THAT?'

'Er, yes, it was further up than I expected; and now, Mrs Williamson, you're going to have to relax, because I can't get my head out of your arse.'

'Forceps . . . scissors . . . coffin . . .'

'OK, Mr Cosgrove, what happens if I press it like that? . . . Right, can someone get him down from the ceiling?'

'Sorry about this shaving thing. Bit embarrassing, isn't it? Particularly for me; I'm the receptionist.'

'OK, so if you could just drop your pants and bend over that bed . . . and we're live on air . . . anyone got a question for this week's arse?'

'Dear God, take this man into your heart so he can live forever beneath your wings.'

'No, it definitely shouldn't be doing that. Quick, get the net – catch it! Catch it!'

'So we take all the stitches out like this, and the wound should support the . . . put them back! Put them back!'

'This gynaecological exam will be done by Frank Stevens, the world's smallest doctor . . . Frank? Frank?'

UNLIKELY THINGS TO SAY
ON A DATE

'I could have sworn it said "nudist" on the dating form.'

'You've probably guessed from the fact that I've just drunk a bottle of whisky that I'm an alcoholic.'

'You used to be a woman? Weird – I used to be a man!'

'To save time, I've written out a list of answers to frequently asked questions.'

'I am so sorry that I misread the signals. Let me put my trousers back on.'

'Your husband used to beat you up? I can relate to that. I used to beat up my ex-wife.'

'Oh, go on, you order a dessert, I'm going to go to the bathroom and sneak out of the window.'

'Thanks very much for this evening. I do have another couple of prospective girlfriends to see, so I'll let you know in a couple of days.'

'I like my penis tickled with a feather duster . . . oh, I see! You mean what do I like for a starter **to eat**.'

'Well, that's a lovely offer, to go home and have you for dessert! It's just that . . . the crème brûlée here does look really good.'

UNLIKELY THINGS TO HEAR ON THE RADIO

'Welcome to *Gardeners' Question Time*, and in response to the first question this week: no, you can't have your ball back.'

'Next, *Woman's Hour*, where today they'll be discussing *blah blah blah blah . . .*'

'Welcome to Classic FM for an hour of smooth, calming classics – interspersed with adverts for Viagra, funerals and the National Trust.'

'Over now to our flying eye . . . '
     'There's a massive tailback on the M25 this morning, as people try to look at my helicopter while driving along.'

'You're listening to Smooth FM . . . oooh, my knackers are so itchy.'

'Welcome to the Radio One Breakfast Show with me, Nick Grimshaw. Our phone-in today is just to let me know there's someone out there listening.'

'Let's go straight to another tune, as our regular elderly DJ seems to have been arrested.'

'Time now for *Book at Bedtime*, brought to you by Gideons International. And once again, it's the Bible.'

'Time now on BBC Radio 2 for *Sound of the Seventies* . . . "Stop that at once, I'm not that kind of girl . . .".'

UNLIKELY CHEESE NAMES

CORNISH INBRED

BISHOP'S KNOB

MERSEYSIDE

REICHSTAG

ATHLETE'S FOOT

GOAT'S TEAT SEEPAGE

SMEGMA BLUE

STINKING SH*T

OFF MILK

FIDDLING BISHOP

UNLIKELY THINGS TO HEAR ON A BUSINESS PROGRAMME

'Time for a look at the stock market . . . Knorr are doing very well, and so are Bisto.'

'And now, the business news. If next door's cat does its business in my garden again, I'm going to flatten it and put it on the barbecue.'

'The pound made a shock rise this morning, as, coincidentally . . . did my penis . . . for once . . . ha ha! Not dead yet!'

'So, David, in light of this fiasco, I'm afraid you're fired . . . no, hang on, that's not enough. Your presentation was so awful, I sentence you to be taken from this place and to a prison and thence to a place of execution, where ye shall be hung by the neck until ye be dead and thereafter buried within the precincts of the prison. May the Lord have mercy on your soul.'
'Thank you for the opportunity, Sir Alan.'

'The dollar continued its downward progress today, just like my f**king tits.'

'Oh my God! I f**king love money. I f**king do. Love it, love it, love it, love it. Let me roll around in it. Oh my God, oh God oh God oh God. Oh yes, oh yes, oh yes!'

THINGS A SPORTS COMMENTATOR
WOULD NEVER SAY

'Look at that! And THAT exposed hairy arse-crack is why
Greco-Roman wrestling is back in the Olympics.'

'Lewis Hamilton completes another lap. That's lap
number . . . er . . . well, it must be – I'll get back to you
on that one.'

'Welcome to the Schools boxing final. And remember,
the bell is a signal for me.'

'Well, I've enjoyed my summer off, time to get the latest
from the matches round the country, starting with
Stuart Hall. Stuart . . . ?'

'All the players are in the bunker. It really is no fun playing
Israeli teams in the Europa League.'

'And as the female golfer approaches her fifteenth, several
1970s DJs can be seen lurking in the bushes.'

'He's approaching the corner at 200 mph – they really are
going to have to check this cyclist for drugs.'

'And that's middle stump cartwheeling out of the ground.
Fantastic aim from Anderson, considering he's peeing
from ten yards away.'

'The shock news in this year's boat race is that it's
Oxford versus Loughborough.'

UNLIKELY THINGS TO HEAR
ON DAYTIME TV

'Welcome to *Sunday Kitchen*, where we'll be eating last night's curry.'

'You're watching Alibi, and funnily enough, you've just rung work and said you've got chicken pox.'

'Welcome to BBC Breakfast. I'm Naga Munchetty.'

'And I'm Charlie Stayt – so yes, you're right, the proper presenters are either ill or in talks with ITV.'

'Welcome to *Wake Up to London* – and now over to Jenny, for the weather and this morning's cyclist casualties.'

'Good morning. It's 7 a.m. on the Horror Channel, and it's time for *Driller Killer*.'

'We would like to apologize to our deaf viewers for the signing during that episode of *Bargain Hunt*. The words "Hello, I'm Tim Wonnacott" were somehow represented by the signs for a bow tie and a wanker gesture.'

'Hiya! It's 4.50 a.m., and you're watching Milkshake on Channel 5. We're here to distract your wide-awake child while you lace their morning Weetabix with Calpol and sedatives.'

'Welcome to the *Daily Politics* show, where I'm asking all our viewers to text in questions for Danny Alexander and Esther McVey . . . come on, text now . . . come on, you three, what else are you doing?'

UNLIKELY THINGS TO READ
IN A ROMANTIC NOVEL

He exploded inside her, like an old jar of rhubarb chutney in a pensioner's fridge.

'Promise you will love me forever and respect me in the morning,' she said, as they threw their kebabs aside and climbed into the skip.

He gazed into her eyes and said, 'Is it better with this lens, or this lens?'

She saw the clothes strewn across the landing – shoes, pants, trousers – and thought to herself, 'Hang on – how did he get his pants off before his trousers?'

It was the gayest costume ball that Pemberley had ever seen. Mr Darcy was dressed as Liberace.

If you're finding the erotic S&M scenes in this book arousing, why not try slamming the book shut on your cock?

He took her slowly in his arms, pulled her towards him gently, and then . . . he shagged her.

She breathed heavily, and fumbled for his manhood. 'This is too big for me,' she gasped, 'and why do you call it a manhood, when it's an anorak?'

'Just because you're older than me, doesn't mean we can't have fun. Now slip out of those Tena pants, and put your teeth in.'

UNLIKELY THINGS TO HEAR
IN HOSPITAL

'Yes, I'm about to do the operation, but I just need to check one thing . . . umm . . . *the thigh bone's connected to the knee bone, the knee bone's connected to the . . .*'

'OK, Mr Simpkins, could I possibly attach these electrodes to your head, take the other and place it so . . . it's alive! It's alive!'

'We've taken your liver out by mistake, but I'm prepared to use its value towards the cost of the operation.'

'Yes, we're going to be filming this operation for Channel 5's *Lethal Procedures*.'

'Well Mrs Hopkins, the good news is we managed to save your husband's good kidney. The bad news is, we threw away the rest of him.'

'No, it is perfectly normal to have a stethoscope grafted on to your anus – and no, I was not drunk!'

'Thank you for the small black grapes, Doctor. Most kind.'
'I didn't give you any small black grapes. Now, where did I leave those hemorrhoids I extracted this morning?'

'Gather round, students. This is how *not* to do a vasectomy.'

'No, don't worry. I changed my name to Shipman. It used to be Mengele.'

'Funnily enough, this will be the last colonoscopy I'll do before my ban comes into effect.'

UNLIKELY THINGS TO READ
IN A DIET BOOK

In this diet, cake, biscuits, sweets and alcohol are all allowed. The catch? It doesn't work.

Lose pounds this way! Day one: eat as much as you like. Day two: have a really big sh*t.

This liquid diet works wonders – drink a bottle of gin, and sleep through at least six meals.

If you want to lose pounds quickly, I recommend online casinos.

Just because you're dieting doesn't mean you can't eat chocolate and cake . . . oh, hang on, yes it does – that's exactly what it means.

I'm following the 5:2 Diet. At about five to, I'm going to have a massive fry-up.

Just remember the handy acronym JSE SMF YFF: Just Stop Eating, So Much Food, You Fat F**k.

This is the same diet that Jennifer Aniston uses. And she's thin, and manically unhappy.

Try putting your food on a smaller plate. You might also need two or three plates.

Now with easy-to-turn pages, for your big, fat, podgy, sausage-fingered hands.

Lose fifteen pounds instantly – by buying this book.

REJECTED QUESTIONS FROM THIS YEAR'S EXAMS

1. If John smuggles 10 ounces of grade-A cocaine with a street value of £10,000 up his arse, what sentence can he expect if he gets caught at the Colombian border?

2. Using negative numbers, plot the Lib Dem share of the vote on this X–Y graph.

3. Showing workings, if Fred = me, explain how Fred was supposed to know that she was under age.

4. If John is bigger than Keith and Keith is bigger than Bill – and Jack is bigger than Keith or Bill, but smaller than Rob, Dean or Phil – then who boasts about his penis the most?

5. Who is the biggest c**t you know, and why?

6. Were you bullied as a child? If yes, give examples, and make them detailed so we can all have a good laugh.

7. Pick up your brushes and paint. Working on your back and using the scaffolding provided, complete the chapel ceiling within five years.

8. Using the animals provided, demonstrate the concept of 'bestiality'.

9. Using only your penis, masturbate.

10. What is wrinkled, yellow and smells of ginger? NB: The answer 'Fred Astaire's middle finger' will result in not only an immediate fail, but also suspension from school.

11. Using only your innate cunning and the knife provided, kill the others before they kill you.

12. Personal Hygiene Exam: Using only the paper provided, wipe your bottom. Please show workings.

13. Did you study hard for this exam? Did you? Really? I didn't. I did nothing. I'm just naturally clever.

14. Cooking Exam Practical, Part 3: Apple Turnover. Turn over your apples now.

15. French: Why are they so annoying?

16. Detective Exam: Where were you last night? Really? Do you have a witness? OK. Punch him, Sarge.

UNLIKELY THINGS TO HEAR IN A WEATHER FORECAST

'Chilly at first, warming up gradually and by morning very pleasant. That's what my bed sheets will be like.'

'For parts of Wales, there'll be 100 per cent humidity – or, as it's also known, flooding.'

'We had a call earlier from a woman worried there might be a tornado on the way. Well, Dorothy in Kansas, let me reassure you.'

'For viewers in Scotland: that big yellow thing in the sky is called the Sun.'

'Phew! I'm sweating like a 1970s DJ.'

'So, with three feet of snow and brilliant skiing conditions, it's going to be another miserable British summer.'

'There's a deep depression over Scotland, just like there is at every World Cup.'

'Conditions rather frosty, down to sub-zero at times. Honestly, you forget one anniversary . . .'

'It should reach 90 degrees by lunchtime – provided I remember to take my mid-morning Viagra.'

UNLIKELY THINGS TO HEAR IN
A PARTY POLITICAL BROADCAST

'We in UKIP are not a one-issue party. It's not just immigration – it's Europe, foreigners, people from overseas . . .'

'I am one of Thatcher's children. And this is my brother, Mark.'

'One potato, two potato, three potato, four. Well, that's the Scottish diet sorted out.'

'As Mayor of London, can I just say I'm fully in favour of fracking . . . oh, it doesn't mean what I thought it did.'

'"Hi. Many people feel we Lib Dems have nothing left to say . . ." That was a party political broadcast on behalf of the Liberal Democrats.'

'They always say two 'Eds are better than one – unless their surnames are Miliband and Balls.'

'And now I'll explain my party's policy using the medium of interpretive dance.'

'Most of the problems with the coalition have been caused by the Liberals . . . Hang on a minute, we *are* the Liberals.'

'We must decide whether we want to be in or out of the constant debate over whether we want to be in or out of Europe.'

EXTRACTS FROM DVDS THAT DIDN'T SELL

'Hello, I'm Rory McIlroy – welcome to my crazy world of golf! Sorry, my world of crazy golf.'

The sensational new drama from America, *Breaking Mad Wirepranos*: it's the series that literally everyone has heard of but no one has watched, except for journalists on the Saturday *Guardian*, who got it for free.

The King's Speech, Special Edition. Remastered by George Lucas, with extra Jabba the Hut scenes added in.

Location, Location, Location box set. Available in shops, right at the back, top shelf, between World Music and the staff toilets.

Peppa Pig: Too Hot for TV – Mummy Pig comes home early and catches Daddy Pig with Madame Gazelle.

Star Wars: The Phantom Menace, Director's Cut. Running time: four and half minutes.

Fast and Furious box set. All the films remastered with an extra dimension, bringing the characterization up to 2D.

Avatar – new edition with over two hours taken out, bringing it down to a snappy five and half hours.

Fireman Sam: After Hours – Sam works as an electrician and male stripper when he should be on call.

'Now, one of the most legendary acts in music: Kraftwerk Unplugged.'

'Thanks for buying this in-depth look at last week's Ashes. That looks like Granny's tooth, here's her hip replacement . . . and I think that gold blob used to be her wedding ring.'

Due to engineering works, this *Thomas the Tank Engine* DVD has been temporarily replaced by a *Bertie the Bus* DVD.

UNLIKELY LINES FROM
A PARENTING MANUAL

No doubt you're feeling anxious, worried and desperate to do the right thing. Great. That's how we make all our money.

The naughty step is a great place for you to get some peace and quiet while your kids destroy your house.

Spare the rod and spoil the child. Luckily, I always carry a spare rod.

If you found the first year hard, every subsequent year is worse. There is no escape.

Slapping can be useful sometimes. It helps keep you awake when you're driving to school.

At the back is a chapter especially for fathers. It's been left blank for you to doodle on.

One fun thing to do before the birth is take a picture of your partner's vagina. It'll never look like that again.

The second birth will be quicker than the first and by the fourth, they'll be coming out like swimmers on a flume.

A regular sleep pattern is essential, so ignore that screaming brat in the next room.

UNLIKELY THINGS TO READ
IN AN OBITUARY

R.I.P. . . . V.A.N. . . . W.I.N.K. . . . OH HANG ON,
IT'S RIP VAN WINKLE.

JOHN'S DEATH IS IN ALL THE NEWSPAPERS TODAY – HE DIED
WHEN HE FELL INTO THE PRINTING PRESS.

SADLY, DESPITE BEING REGARDED AS ONE OF THE
CLEVEREST MEN EVER TO GRADUATE FROM CAMBRIDGE,
DICK LITTLEWILLY-POOCOCK WAS NEVER REALLY TAKEN
SERIOUSLY DURING HIS TEACHING CAREER.

A GREAT FATHER, A WONDERFUL HUSBAND, BUT A RUBBISH
HANG-GLIDER.

HE LITERALLY SHAT HIMSELF TO DEATH.

HE WAS ALWAYS A TALL MAN – AT LEAST, UNTIL HE FELL
FROM THE TOP OF THE SHARD AND MADE HIMSELF
CONSIDERABLY MORE 'COMPACT'.

WHATEVER NELSON MANDELA ACHIEVED IN HIS POLITICAL
CAREER, HE WILL MAINLY BE REMEMBERED AS A CRIMINAL
WHO WAS RIGHTLY JAILED FOR HIS ACTIONS.

THE EXACT TIME OF HIS DEATH WAS UNCERTAIN, AS I HAD
TO DROP THIS IN THE LAST WEEKEND POST ON THE
JOURNEY OVER TO HIS FLAT.

RIP, A PIONEER OF SOCIAL NETWORKING. #SADFACE

UNLIKELY SMALL ADS

Mobile phone for sale. Please email, as phone doesn't work properly.

FOR SALE: unused wedding dress, size 28. Some tear-stains. And gravy.

For the sale, teaching of the big English to the book. Writings, Discs of Compact, all to be includings.

Do you know the way to San Jose? Can you tell me the way to Amarillo? Are you 24 Hours from Tulsa? Not sure? Then compass for sale. Tiny. Used to be in shoe.

Bottle of Lidl own-brand brown sauce. Can't read sell-by date, but may be OK.

Sperm for sale. Almost new. About a minute old. Bring own test tube or tissue.

Sh*t for sale. It's everywhere. Make me an offer . . . please . . . it won't stop. I think I might be very ill. As new. Would make great manure. In fact, for an extra £2, I'll come and stand in your garden.

Original Van Gogh, *Sunflowers*, for sale. £7 ONO. No questions asked – it's real, honestly.

Large bottle of milk, just smashed. Milk for sale. Buyer collects. Act really fast. Offer ends in about thirty seconds. Must like milk mixed with glass and/or stuff under fridge. Call now. No crying.

The Complete Works of Shakespeare. Signed by author. £45 because of a bit of water damage when the bath overflowed.

Piece of toast. Nearly new – only one bite out of it. Offer ends Thursday.

Packet of Trebor. Mint condition.

FOR SALE: Mozart's piano. Call Ken Mozart now.

FOR SALE: Frosty the Snowman nose. No, it isn't just a carrot. Also original eyes, buttons and scarf. All genuine, from the movie. What? It was a cartoon? OK, picture of Frosty the Snowman's nose for sale.

FOR SALE: Picture of my cock. Scaled bids only by Thursday.

FOR SALE: Photocopies of my arse. Not great quality. See Sotheby's catalogue for details.

Packet of Murray Mints for sale. No need to hurry.

Buddhist Unicorn for sale . . . well, OK, it's a stickleback now, but it was definitely a unicorn in a previous life.

Semen wanted. First come, first served.

Child for sale. Buyer collects. Go to St John's Primary School, and say you're 'Steven's dad'.

Salmon for sale. Caught two days ago, comes in own jar. Possibly dead. Thinking about it, it could be a minnow, to be honest; anyway, would make a great conversation piece: e.g., 'Is that dead?' 'Not sure. Could be.' 'Horrible smell, though.' 'Yeah.'

UNLIKELY THINGS TO HEAR
ON A MEDICAL SHOW

'That penis takes the biscuit. I mean, literally, it's just taken a biscuit off my plate.'

'You don't need to give me a round of applause, sir. What I actually said was "You've got the *clap*".'

'Welcome to Kill or Cure – this week, we're off to Switzerland.'

'I don't care if you are Minister for Health, Mr Hunt, you can't perform open heart surgery.'

'This kind of deformity is impossible to treat, but you have to agree, it makes f**king great telly.'

'In my opinion, it could be a slight curvature of the upper spine. But that's just a hunch.'

'Well, normally a spoonful of sugar helps the medicine go down; but in this case, it seems to have counteracted the insulin.'

'This is a very interesting case. I keep my stethoscope in it.'

'There's nothing at all wrong with your breasts. I don't normally like female doctors, but with you I'll make an exception.'

'Open wide and say "Arhhh". As I thought: you're a pirate.'

UNLIKELY LINES TO HEAR IN *STAR TREK*

'It's a weird, asexual creature, fluent in Klingon.
Exactly the sort of viewer we want for our
new space movie.'

'Captain, the disappointing 3D effects are draining
the central energy reserves.'

'Aaah! I've been shot in the eye with a laser!
But the good news is, I've now got 20:20 vision.'

'Captain – we're out of milk again.'

'You Vulcans – you come over here, taking our jobs . . .'

'Live long and . . . you'll eventually be cast
in the remake.'

'It's chaos down there, Captain! Aliens have just invaded
the Labour conference, and asked to be taken to
their leader.'

'Captain, there's a Jehovah's Witness at the airlock –
are we in?'

'This planet has a complicated system of rings,
but I'm sure if we go round once more I'll be able
to find the turn-off.'

'I've got bad news for you, Kirk: although you're
only 25 now, eventually you will look like
William Shatner.'

'The spaceship went at warp factor four, Captain,
and now it's warped.'

'I know it's not logical, Spock. But I honestly reckon,
if I spend ten quid, I can win the Euromillions.'

'Let's give that planet a miss. It's inhabited by
some sort of dragon that seems to be dishing out soup
to a bunch of pink knitted rats.'

'We've identified those blobs on the radar: mayonnaise.
Sorry about that.'

'I have something to tell you, Captain Kirk.'
'OK, Spock, I'm all ears.'
'Don't take the piss.'

'Beam me down, Scottie.'
'Certainly, Captain. Is it a day return or a Super Saver
you're after?'

'There's something caught in the tractor beam, Captain!
Oh, it's a tractor.'

'We've landed on a planet of infinite beauty with untold
resources. Let's start shooting everyone.'

'Remember: if we can't get any Unobtanium, we'll make
do with some Relativelyeasytogetium.'

UNLIKELY THINGS TO READ
IN A ROMANTIC NOVEL

Reader, I tugged him off.

'Darling, you are one of the few men I can trust, so can you hold my drink while I go for a dump?'

'My secret,' he said, 'is that I am a vampire, and that once a month I must taste human flesh.' 'Oh, that's OK,' she said. 'As long as you're not a member of UKIP.'

'Why, Mr Darcy! That's the first time I've been fingered in a car park.'

He gazed at her, she gazed at him, and he said, 'Mmmff, mmmffff,' through the gaffer tape.

'You really are the most ravishing beauty,' said Boris, as he gazed into the mirror.

She smouldered gently at the end of the bar – her hair was on fire.

'Don't worry about it,' she murmured. 'At your age it's quite common to get no satisfaction, Mick.'

As he looked into her eyes his heart began to pound, and he felt a tingling sensation. What a terrible time to have a major coronary.

'Fancy a coffee?' she said. He suspected his luck was in and began to undress, at which point he was thrown out of Starbucks.

UNLIKELY THINGS TO HEAR
AT A PARTY CONFERENCE

'Quick – dodge round to the left, or we'll
be stuck behind Eric Pickles at the
breakfast buffet.'

'I've booked the entire Tory cabinet into the
nearest decent hotel to Blackpool I could get.
We're in the Ritz Piccadilly, London.'

'The phrase is "Tory cuts" – it doesn't have
an 'n' in it.'

'I say to you: put your trust in the Lord,
rise up from your wheelchair and walk. And that
concludes this health policy speech.'

'Please welcome the man who's done more for
the Tory party than any other leader –
Ed Miliband.'

'We must try and energize people to become
involved in grass-roots politics, we must
speak directly to the nation . . . but first we
must find the caretaker to unlock the
conference hall.'

'We'll reduce taxes, we'll increase spending
and – Hang on, can I start again? I think I've
got them the wrong way round.'

'They come round here, take our jobs – that's
why the BNP says "don't vote UKIP".'

'I've followed Nigel Farage's advice. We didn't want
a family of Romanians living next door to us,
so we've moved here from Romania.'

'Don't forget, Comrades: who created this bloody mess
we've got to clear up? That's right – it was us.'

'I'm Nick Clegg, and I'd like to ask you
an important question: would you like to buy
the *Big Issue*?'

'Let me say this to the Romanian and Polish
immigrants in this country: can I have a
flat white and a croissant?'

UNLIKELY THINGS TO READ IN A WILL

I, William Henderson, being of sound mind and wibble . . .

It's important that you take this down precisely, word for word: I, Albert Higgins, being of sound mind and body . . . ooh, cramp, f**k, cramp, cramp, cramp!

I have asked my solicitor to summon you all here . . . because my murderer is somewhere in this room.

Help, help, prise the lid off, quick – I'm trapped in here!

Being enfeebled by illness, I am recording my final will and testament on tape. I leave all my worldly goods and monies to my [tape recorder clicks] solicitor . . .

I'd like to leave my wife . . . but it's too late now, I'm dead.

I'd like to leave my collection of mistreated pit bulls to my ex-wife.

I have left all my worldly goods in a hollow tree. But where? My first is in tiger, but not in grit . . .

Contrary to popular belief, you CAN take it all with you, if you do as I have done and convert it all into banknotes and have yourself cremated yesterday. Screw you all, with your cheap second-rate nursing home!

THINGS YOU WON'T HEAR
IN A SCIENCE DOCUMENTARY

'And the fundamental building blocks of nature are created . . . by God. Praise be.'

'First there was the Big Bang, and just seconds later I was swapping insurance details with the other driver.'

'This is the periodic table. I keep it just by this occasional chair.'

'A lot of people have difficulty understanding neurological medical techniques. But hey, it's not brain surgery.'

'I'm here for two reasons: (a) to teach you about the origins of the universe, and (b) because Brian Cox is now too expensive.'

'After a long time, Man was able to walk upright, and he eventually made it home from the pub, though he felt like sh*t the next day.'

'Let's get rid of a couple of myths about science – starting with dinosaurs and Darwin.'

'The universe began with a Big Bang . . . as, indeed, did we all.'

[*Falsetto voice*] 'Helium is my favourite element. I can't speak of it highly enough.'

'This whole magical story sprang into life when the producer asked me, Professor Brian Cox, if I had any old guff I'd like to put on telly.'

'So, if we harness the power of every wind turbine in the country . . . we can just about get this light bulb to flicker.'

'Right, so I've got my test tube – all I need now is a copy of *Razzle*, and I'm ready to donate.'

'This astonishing array of chemicals in liquid solution has a name – Sunny Delight.'

'So that's the latest on the round-the-world flight by the sunlight-powered solar plane – it crashed when it got to Scotland.'

'This is the very latest in wind power: to heat your house efficiently in winter, just set light to your own farts.'

'A pound of uranium, half a kilo of thorium hydroxide, 200 milligrams of nitric acid . . . You know, I'm really not sure about this dish, Heston.'

'One hundred hamsters can generate enough light for a four-bedroomed house – don't put them in a wheel, just chuck 'em on the fire.'

'These power stations are perfectly safe, as long as we follow the ratio of three parts uranium to one part plutonium. Or is it the other way round?'

'We don't know the exact extent of Prince Philip's surgery, but we do know that he now wishes to be known as "Prince Cybernetic Killer Robot the First".'

THINGS A SPORTS COMMENTATOR
WOULD NEVER SAY

'Let's have a close-up look at exactly what grip Monty Panesar is using – no, too slow, he's zipped up.'

'And just two years on, there's an amazing competition going on here at the Olympic Stadium: two pigeons fighting over a chip.'

'And as they dip for the line . . . I think Tulisa has got there first.'

'Through the chicane, then it's round the long left-hander . . . a quick swerve round George Michael, lying in the middle of the road . . .'

'The Bulgarian has got the gold medal! He lifted it out of Chris Hoy's pocket when he wasn't looking.'

'And that's disappointing: what started out as a disputed stumping between India and Pakistan has developed into all-out nuclear war.'

'Welcome back to the Tour de France, where Chris Froome has burned through the field like a Lance Armstrong urine sample through the bottom of a test tube.'

'A strong first leg, less successful on the second leg: I think that's the last we'll see of Heather Mills ice-skating.'

He's got a six, to go with his four . . . welcome back to All-Star Monopoly, the only sport still shown by the BBC.'

'And we'll take a break there from the radio commentary at Aintree, as I've dropped one of my coconut shells.'

UNLIKELY THINGS TO HEAR
ON THE RADIO

'Welcome to Hospital Radio. Here's a message for Mary, who was brought in with a heart attack: they've found a bed for you now, so you can leave this studio.'

'And now for tonight's *Book at Bedtime, They Were Murdered While They Slept*.'

'For commentary on the big game at Manchester City – over to Stuart Hall in Pentonville.'

'And now for the traffic report, where you are: there's severe congestion around the kitchen doorway, because Mum's just taken a cake out of the oven.'

'Time now for *Thought for the Day* . . . Hmmmm. And now back to the studio.'

'And now on Radio 4, it's time for the pips – yes, the most boring episode yet of *Gardeners' Question Time*.'

'Welcome to Jazz Radio: on terrestrial, on digital, online – but most likely not on at all.'

'Now on *Women's Hour*, the programme for strong, independent women: how to knit a scarf, do your own smear test and ice a cake – remember to use a different spatula! Then back to nasty old politics.'

'And now for *Book at Bedtime* – this week it's Brian Blessed's autobiography, read by the author himself.'

UNLIKELY THINGS FOR
A VET TO SAY

'Good news! I've managed to cut your pet mouse free from that length of fabric he was caught up in . . . oh, your pet *bat*?'

'This one has really got me scratching my head. I just wish I'd washed my hand after sticking it up your dog's arse.'

'So, three tablets of ketamine – that should get me through another day of people's f**king pets.'

'The bad news is that your tropical fish didn't make it. But the good news – sushi for lunch.'

'You're not going to believe it, but this actually *is* a dead parrot.'

'That's cute – your dog is sitting up and begging – but I'm going to cut his balls off anyway.'

'This new neutering device really is the dog's bollocks.'

'Your cat is healed – see, *this* is why I became a vet. Not just because I failed proper medical school.'

'Good news! I managed to cut your pet dog free from that hoover extension he'd got stuck on the end of his face . . . oh, your pet *anteater*?'

'I've examined your stick insect, and I'm going to prescribe a visit to an optician. This is a stick.'

'That's right, Timmy – your doggie will be going to a farm in the country, where its corpse will be cremated and used as fertilizer.'

'We've amputated your cat's back legs, and replaced them with wheels – we didn't need to, but it'll look hilarious on YouTube.'

'Yes, that steamroller may have put paid to Mrs Tiggywinkle – but on the plus side, you now have an excellent Frisbee to remember her by.'

'Just keep that plastic collar in place for a week or so – not to protect the stitches, just to cover up the real botch job I made of it.'

'I've wrapped your duck in something special – pancakes and hoisin sauce . . . delicious!'

'I'm afraid I've had to put down all four dozen of your pet minks. But the good news is, I've solved the problem of what to get my wife for her birthday.'

'After six months caring for this badger, he's finally well enough to be released into the wild. Off you go! [*shotgun blast*] Oh . . .'

'I can confirm that your hamster died while taking exercise – yes, he fell asleep at the wheel.'

'You have got a lovely shiny coat, haven't you, mmm, yes he has, yes he has! Eh boy? And so has your dog.'

'It's quite ironic that your cat is called Sooty – as I'm just about to put my hand up his arse.'

'We've re-attached his nose, given him a new car, and had to amputate one paw. But apart from that, Lucky's fine.'

'I'm afraid the operation went wrong and Tiddles didn't make it. But on the plus side – you have got a new pyjama case!'

'Put it this way: if Rover was human, I would be recommending a one-way ticket to Switzerland.'

UNLIKELY LINES FROM A PARENTING MANUAL

If you do like to throw your child lovingly into the air, turn off the ceiling fan first.

Encourage your wife during labour, though references to John Hurt and Alien are not helpful.

It's important that you set your children clear boundaries. Fence off their bedroom, and tell them they can't come out.

I recommend a fresh bottle just before bedtime – that should be enough wine for you to sleep through all the crying.

Mushed-up, pureed vegetables . . . are all you'll be able to eat after not sleeping for three weeks.

You should be able to reason with a child. But if not, chocolates and television should do it.

You may want to avoid having another baby too quickly, so remember that a useful form of contraception is . . . having a young baby.

Remember, your child may want to sleep in your bed, which is fine. Because then you can go and sleep in theirs.

Always make sure, when your child is on the Internet, that the person they're talking to is who they say they are. To check, why not pretend to be one of their school friends?

For parents of toddlers, stamping, screaming and tantrums are commonplace, and the kids sometimes do the same.

UNLIKELY THINGS TO SAY
ON A DATE

'I've never had a first date by Skype before, but if you're ever near the Ecuadorian embassy . . .'

'I've got a good feeling about this date. I've met all nine of my wives here.'

'Here we are – beer for me, and a vodka and Rohypnol for you. Red Bull, sorry.'

'Why don't you unzip the gimp mask and tell me about yourself?'

'I'm sorry. Whenever I think about my wife's death I start crying. I still find it really funny.'

'If you don't like it, I can ask the violinist to go away. But these Albert Hall tickets were quite expensive.'

'Let's go somewhere a bit quieter . . . and lonely . . . and not over-looked by any meddling do-gooders.'

'Well, you seem like a nice man, I'm glad I came along to . . . marry me!'

'Oh, you've finished your pudding. Er – did you not notice a ring in it anywhere?'

'Will you make me the happiest man in the world . . . and pay for one of these bloody dinners?'

UNLIKELY THINGS TO READ
IN A MAINTENANCE MANUAL

If the pilot goes out, try to sober up the co-pilot.

If the pressure rises to a dangerous level, calm down, leave the room, have a big scotch and get a professional in.

Stick a knife in it, wiggle it about a bit and then see what happens.

Bleeding radiators – a cry often heard when they break down.

Before you set off for your first journey on your new unicycle, check that in some way you are dressed like a twat.

Your new boiler has been tested to give you years of trouble-free service – three years, in fact, until the guarantee wears out.

If you unplugged the shredder before clearing the blockage, go to page 47. If you didn't, go to hospital.

Ask someone to check your indicators are working. If they say 'Yes they are, no they're not, yes they are, no they're not', punch them in the face.

If the overheating sign comes on, remember: this is a nuclear power plant. RUN LIKE F**K.

UNLIKELY THINGS TO READ
IN A DRIVING MANUAL

It's important to keep below 70. Any older than that, and you shouldn't really be on the road.

If you are in a road with a sleeping policeman – bang on their car window and wake them up.

Keep an eye on your speed, and if you get stopped by the police, stash it up your arse.

Hold the wheel in the '10 to 2' position with your knees – that way you can still juggle your coffee and pasty.

Hand signals are important in letting other drivers know when you're pulling out, when you're giving way, and when you think they're a massive cock.

Remember, as you go past 70 you do tend to veer to the right. So try not to mouth obscenities at foreign drivers.

Remember the different lane uses on the M25. The slow lane is for parking, the middle lane is for beeping your horn as you sit completely stationary, and the fast lane is for picnics.

When approaching a rider on a horse,
approach as slowly and quietly as possible.
At the last moment, rev your engine and
beep the horn. It's hilarious.

Try and slow down when you approach
bumps in the road (or cyclists, as they're
better known).

Points to remember: 30 for a cyclist,
20 for a pedestrian, 5 for a hedgehog.

Don't forget the routine: mirror, cocaine, snort.

Check your mirror for people behind you.
Wait till there are some, then start dogging.

THINGS A WIMBLEDON COMMENTATOR WOULD NEVER SAY

'Murray has hit the ball down the tram lines . . . and it's hit a tram!'

'Over to Hawkeye – no, still no clue as to whether he's in or out. So the Cliff Richard debate continues . . .'

'New balls! It's very painful perched up here in the umpire's chair.'

'Look at that Mexican wave! His name's Pedro, and he's just spotted the TV camera pointing at him.'

'Amazing! With this latest video technology, I can see right into the ladies' changing rooms.'

'Let's go now to court four, where I believe another BBC presenter is being sentenced to prison.'

'Pippa Middleton is here, and people are craning to get a look at the arse. Yes, she's brought her current boyfriend with her.'

'There's a grunt – another grunt – and another grunt. The umpire really is enjoying Maria Sharapova bending over to pick up the ball.'

'As a former British tennis player, it's completely obvious to me what Andy Murray should do, in a way that I was never able to do myself.'

'Rafael Nadal there, picking at the fluff on his balls. Soon he'll be out of the shower and on the court.'

UNLIKELY THINGS TO HEAR
IN *DOCTOR WHO*

'I think the BBC must be using product placement, because the Doctor has just been attacked by the Honey Monster.'

'Doctor! Someone seems to have broken into the TARDIS and left lots of little cards! 'New in Town, Pre-Op, Filthy, genuine photo' – whatever can it mean?'

'Right, I've killed that Cyberman. Now, do the bits go in the red recycling bin, or the green one?'

'I knew I shouldn't have left the TARDIS door unlocked – a tramp's come in and shat on the console.'

'We're in one of the most dangerous places I've ever been: it's the BBC television studios, and it's 1972.'

'They are the nicest breasts I've ever seen, but I should probably tell you that I'm not that sort of doctor.'

'Bad news: the composer's written very quiet music this week, so you're going to have to try and say some vaguely convincing dialogue.'

'Looks like it's time for the Doctor to regenerate into a cheaper actor.'

'Oh my God, we're locked out of the TARDIS – oh no, my mistake – I should have pushed, not pulled.'

'I think that sea monster came out of the English Channel – it's got a condom on its head.'

'Doctor, you're regenerating! You're . . . hang on, you've turned into David Tennant again.'

'Where's the sonic screwdriver? It's in the sonic toolbox, where it's supposed to be, in the cupboard under the sonic stairs!'

UNLIKELY PERSONAL ADS

Man, GSOH, NLI (Good Sense Of Humour, No Longer Infectious).

Frail, elderly pensioner would like to meet man with GCH (Gas Central Heating).

Cross-eyed? Buck-toothed? Bad breath? Ha ha ha! Loser!

Seven-foot-two, one-eyed albino hunchback, with webbed toes and banana-shaped birthmark, seeks similar for relationship.

Man from the 1970s seeks woman with great big b-b-b-b-b-boots . . . oooh, Matron . . . *boing*! Wah, wah, wah, waaah . . . zoiks! Aye caramba!

Man with no ambition seeks woman to do nothing. Maybe less.

Serial killer, looking for love . . . or am I? Don't die wondering.

Man with no ladder seeks woman with very long arms to help change light bulbs.

Are you looking for something different? Something special? Well, f**k off, then.

Impatient man seeks woman with GSOH who takes . . . oh, I can't be bothered with this.

Are you a beautiful, curvaceous woman with golden hair, strong thighs and full, ruby lips . . . ooh, sorry, I've just come.

Man with masturbation obsession seeks understanding woman prepared to handle my issues. Sorry, that should have read 'tissues'.

Are you up for it? Are you? Are you? Are you? Come on! I'm asking: are you? If you are, then be like all the others and don't reply/call the police.

Othello seeks his Desdemona – for love and Moor.

In for a penny? In for a pound? I'd rather be in for a penny at the moment, if that's all right with you.

Premature ejaculator seeks understanding wo . . . oh, sorry about that.

Man seeks woman who loves lying on her back with her legs open, because I've smashed my vase. (p.s. Other jokes from 1973 are available on request.)

Bonjour. Un homme WLTM une femme for a bit of French oral. It's on Tuesday afternoon, in the ROSLA block.

'Postman' Pat seeks woman who likes it in a van. Must like cats and dogging, and love a man with a bulging package (but very small penis).

Come and rescue me from my desert island of loneliness. Let's surf the waves on a raft of love and never run aground. Call Dave, Broadmoor.

COMMERCIALS THAT NEVER MADE IT TO AIR

And now the science: you're ugly. You need this make-up.

Need a new pubic wig? Go to comparethemerkin.com!

The odds of adverts for at least three different betting companies appearing in this half-time break are on-screen . . . now.

We take the very finest tuna and salmon chunks, and while millions starve around the world, we waste them on a f**king cat.

Farmhouse stew: now with real badger.

Yahama 500: handles country roads unbelievably well for a small digital piano.

You've heard of Tesco Finest and Sainsbury's Taste the Difference – we now bring you the Lidl 'Less Sh*t' range.

Unlimited minutes, unlimited texts, unlimited music downloads with extra-loud external speakers: our new 'twat on the train' tariff.

Captain Birdseye's new beefburger – because we've run out of fish in the sea.

After two weeks, there won't be a single trace of dandruff – because all your hair will have fallen out.

This product has not been tested on animals to check its effectiveness, but it has been tested on animals for a laugh.

Two extra-large bottles for the price of 29 pence . . . because you're worth it.

New anti-wrinkle cream for men. Your scrotum will never have looked so smooth.

Lipstick and blusher: perfect for that first date. Assuming he's even looking at your face.

Because I've convinced myself I'm worth it, even though I know I'm a worthless harlot.

This product gives me glossy, shiny hair, and a lovely cold, wet nose . . . oh, hang on, it's for dogs.

This contains fructoliposomes, DFA peptochromotides, and other polymadeupotones.

Forget all those tooth whiteners – try our revolutionary new gum darkeners.

This new fake tan really is the latest fashion trend. Yes, the future's bright: the future's orange.

UNLIKELY THINGS TO HEAR
ON A MEDICAL SHOW

'This is a £20,000, top-of-the-range scientific microscope. What doctors have to do is work out why this man in casualty has got it shoved up his arse.'

'The doctor has in his hand a prescription for a combination of Valium and Temazepam. Having swallowed them, he can face going back on duty.'

'Alex now weighs 54 stone. Sadly, the treatment he so urgently needs is being delayed because the doctors can't stop laughing.'

'The nurse gives Mr Johnson the bad news. He'll be dead by morning – unless he agrees to stop pressing the emergency buzzer and interrupting her dinner.'

'It is an extremely ugly-looking growth. On the plus side, he's got somewhere to balance his teacup.'

'The bad news, Mr Henderson, is that That's Life isn't on any more, because your genitals look just like tomatoes.'

'That cancerous goitre means that you've got about six months to live – so, to cheer you up, I've drawn a smiley face on it.'

'Good news – the furry growth coming out of your stomach is nothing to worry about. It was just a cat that had been crushed between your folds of flesh.'

'I'll speak up so you can hear me, Mr Cameron: you appear to have your head stuck up your arse.'

THINGS YOU WOULDN'T HEAR
ON A DIY SHOW

'Hello, I'm Nick Knowles, I'm a bit of a
heart-throb, and I've not had to do it myself
for quite a while.'

'Well, we've successfully cut that wood using
a power saw. I think that calls for a high three.'

'This is going to take a lot of screwing – so we'll
take a break for the ads, while I get to know
the new make-up girl a bit better.'

'Today I'll be making a bed. I've already got wood
. . . so I'd better hurry up and get on with it.'

'Now that you've worked out the precise
measurements for your bookcase, look in the
brochure to see if IKEA do one.'

'While building your gym, you'll find this
chipboard is the perfect place to put your chips.'

'It may have been clumsy and carried out
by amateurs, but the assassination of Princess
Diana will fascinate the *Daily Express* for years
to come.'

'Now I need a large plane. I'm going to the Caribbean while I get a bloke in to finish the kitchen.'

'And if you carefully align both the holes . . . one in front of the other . . . you can see that you've drilled through both thumbs.'

'And there we are: a large plastic storage bin, into which you can put all the bits of the wardrobe you f**ked up last week.'

'When you've finished drilling the hole, make sure it's thoroughly sanded down and varnished. You don't want to get splinters when you stick your cock through it.'

UNLIKELY EXERCISE TIPS

Jerk! Jerk! Jerk! Why'd you buy the DVD if you know
you'll never watch it? Useless jerk!

For firmer muscles, try coating your entire body in
quick-drying varnish.

The only way to lose weight is skipping – skipping lunch,
skipping breakfast and skipping dinner.

Fitness is diet and exercise. Drink five litres of
spiced cabbage water, and you'll find yourself doing more
squat thrusts than you thought possible.

Men: watch this DVD and you'll soon have
powerful, rippling biceps and muscular forearms.
It's Holly Willoughby in a low-cut frock.

Do you want a flat stomach? Then shove this book down
the front of your trousers.

Do you want rock-hard buns? Then go to Greggs
at five o'clock in the afternoon.

Gradually increase the distance. After three years,
you should find that the two parties in the Coalition
have almost nothing in common at all.

Make extra time to exercise by getting off the train
to work one stop earlier. After you've been late five days
in a row and have lost your job, you'll have loads of
time to keep fit.

UNLIKELY THINGS TO HEAR AT A FUNERAL

'Could whoever that is stop knocking? I'm trying to do the eulogy.'

'Seeing as it's a chilly day, we thought we'd do the cremation first.'

'We laid him to rest in his favourite spot. It's what he would have wanted – second only to not dying.'

'A keen ecologist, we now lay him to rest . . . Does he go in the blue recycling bin, or the red one?'

'He was an almost fanatical believer in recycling. All I would say is, don't eat the "ham" at the buffet.'

'Brian wanted to be buried with his favourite cat. It was a bugger trying to nail the lid down, with it trying to jump out.'

'I didn't know John very well, but I've collected together a few facts about his life from the Internet. He was either the finest downhill skier Morocco has ever produced, or the most gifted lyrical poet in 15th-century Italy.'

'His remains have been scattered to the four corners of the park. What a car accident that was.'

'Dearly beloved, we gather here to mourn Ben Elton's latest sitcom.'

'We now commit his body to be cremated. Everyone please take a jacket potato each, and follow me outside.'

'I'm afraid there's been a dreadful mix-up over Noel Edmonds' burial arrangements. He's in one of these coffins – I'd like to ask his widow which of the fifteen she'd like to open first.'

UNLIKELY THINGS TO HEAR IN COURT

'My client comes from a broken family. Yes, I know he broke it by murdering his mother.'

'I was proceeding in an easterly direction, in my squad car, when I was pulled over and arrested for impersonating a policeman.'

'I will remind you that it is usual practice to call, "all rise for the judge", not yell, "Who's the Daddy?"'

'Ladies and gentlemen of the jury, I ask you – I beg you – to stop playing Candy Crush on your iPhones for one second, and listen to the f**king case.'

'No, no, don't panic. I'm only putting this black cloth on my head because it's raining and I'm popping outside for a fag. Sorry.'

'Just because these courtroom proceedings are being televised doesn't mean we will make any changes to procedure. Now, I sentence you to . . . [heart beat sound effect] . . . six months.'

'If killing a man, chopping up his body and stuffing him down a sewer makes me guilty . . . then yes, I am guilty.'

'As your lawyer, it pains me to say that we've lost. Well, I say "we". I've got a drinks party tonight, and then dinner with my wife. You're going to prison.'

'This is the worst case of mistaken identity I've ever encountered; I actually came here to read the meter.'

'You will be tried by twelve of your peers – or at least, twelve people not clever enough to get out of jury service.'

'In the case of Regina versus Viagra, all be upstanding.'

UNLIKELY THINGS TO HEAR
IN CHURCH

'Hang on – with all these people, we'll have to
put out extra seats!'

'I now declare you husband and husband.
You may now bum the groom.'

'Put your money away – the roof is fine.'

'News of the organ repair fund, and I'm delighted to
say that our alcoholic Vicar has finally
received his new liver.'

'And Jesus, of course, preached a doctrine of love,
except of course for anyone who disagrees even
slightly with anything we believe.'

'And if anyone has just cause as to why this . . .
abomination between two men should be prevented,
join me . . .'

'I'd like to apologize for last week's Christian rock band,
who threw the font through the stained-glass window.'

'This is a very high-class church – I've never seen a
communion wine list before.'

'I'm pleased for the gentleman in the congregation's
joyful response. But those are hymn numbers,
and not the result of tonight's lottery.'

UNLIKELY THINGS TO HEAR
ON A TV COOKERY SHOW

'This is the best tart I've ever seen, and I think I'm going to leave my wife for her.'

'Now on *Hairy Bikers*, we show you how to cook low-sugar food to combat the diabetes you developed following our recipes over the last ten years.'

'Look at that. Pukka! That's what a pig's arsehole will do, if you squeeze lemon juice on it.'

'I'm Antony Worrall-Thompson. So, that's the cheese, butter and eggs, and if I can get out of the shops with all that up my jumper, I'll be laughing.'

'We're the Hairy Bikers, and the first thing we must do tonight is grease the baking tray.' [*Wipes tray on head*]

'At the River Cottage this week, I've got fish and squid on the table. The floods have been really bad.'

'Mary is now going to eat the tart. Rich, crumbly, with a flaky bottom, she's been a top baker for decades.'

'There you have it, the Hairy Bikers' Irish Stew. Let me just . . . spit this clump of hair out.'

UNLIKELY THINGS FOR
A CRICKET COMMENTATOR TO SAY

'The bowler's Holding, the batsman's Vagina.'

'That ball has sailed right over the rope,
and it's – ow, f**k!'

'That's 2 for 99, the best-value coffee in the ground.'

'That's 299 for 1, the worst-value ice creams ever.'

'The reassuring *thwack* of leather against willow . . .
and after my spanking session, it's down to Lords for
the cricket.'

'A glorious sight here at Lords: cricketers in white
coming out on one side, women being refused entry
on the other.'

'That's a six followed by another six.
If that doesn't get me £200 and past go, nothing will.'

'As they close the roof, we can't help thinking it's
a little low . . . oh, I see, the covers are on.'

'He's hit that ball down to cow corner, where
it's hit a cow.'

UNLIKELY LINES
FROM A PARENTING MANUAL

Little treats can be used as a reward. Once they've got dressed for school, why not treat yourself to a glass of wine?

Sometimes the best way to stop a baby crying is to send it to an orphanage.

Obviously the first question to be faced once you've had twins is: what has that done to your vagina?

This happens a lot. Get used to it. Dry the tears, stop the crying, clean up the wee and poo, and send your husband to the spare room.

Nothing that a swift kick up the arse won't solve.

Can you show a child too much love? Yes. So stop it. It's going to grow up into a f**king monster.

Once you've had babykins, then you might find hubby rejects you for an itsy-bitsy time . . . particularly if you talk like that.

Nothing that a night in a dark cellar with no food won't solve.

The best way to deal with an embarrassing public tantrum is to fight fire with fire – though obviously make sure you put the child out before causing any real damage.

Chapter 23: OK, so you've read all our advice. There is a second option. Don't have kids. Think of the holidays. Think of the lie-ins. Think of the free time and the money . . .

UNLIKELY THINGS TO HEAR
ON A CAR PROGRAMME

'And I'm clearly in the wrong gear . . . I've had this jacket for years, and these stonewashed jeans really are too tight.'

'That's a terrible car crash Richard Hammond has been in. I don't imagine that Saturday-night entertainment show will be recommissioned.'

'Sporting a spare tyre, and with a few miles on the clock, Jeremy Clarkson is back for a new series of *Top Gear*.'

'The dashboard is minimalist and the steering wheel is removable – oh no, hang on, I'm facing the wrong way.'

'The results are in for women's favourite car of the year, and it's . . . a red one.'

'We take a moment away from cars now for our weekly five-minute bullying of James May.'

'Up next – it's thrills all the way, as we test the latest in-car air fresheners.'

'Just whose wife have I been test-driving this week?'

'It took over 200 horsepower and maximum torque ratio, but we finally managed to get Jeremy Clarkson's jeans on.'

UNLIKELY THINGS TO SAY
ON A DATE

'Bagsie the bathroom first in the morning.'

'A bottle of the Chablis, please; and do you want something to drink, love?'

'No wine for me, I'm on super-strength antibiotics.'

'I've been unlucky with dates recently. My last three all went missing on their way home.'

'Do you want garlic bread? Do you want a side salad? Do you want children?'

'Why hasn't someone snapped me up by now? It's because I'm a complete bastard.'

'Then Darth Vader would grab an underling by the throat, like this . . .'

'I like you – you remind me of my mother. Can we have sex?'

'It's great to finally meet you! Up to now I've just had those secret photos I took on the Tube.'

'Let's get the pleasantries out of the way. My name's John – and do you mind sleeping in the wet patch?'

'I've never met a woman on a website before, particularly not eBay.'

UNLIKELY THINGS TO HEAR
A FOOTBALL MANAGER SAY

'So we've lost a few games. It's not like I'm going to lose my job.'

'What are the crowd shouting? I'm getting *what* in the morning?'

'What? Just cos they got that little round thing in that net more times than us, we lost?'

'Wayne presented an eloquent and reasoned argument about his plans. He said "Me wanna go play Chelsea".'

'The first thing I had to do was lower the wage bill, so I sacked the tea lady.'

'OK, so we were knocked out of the cup by Accrington Stanley; at least that leaves us free to be sh*t in the league.'

'We started the game with a minute's silence – followed by 89 minutes' silence. We're just not getting any fans in nowadays.'

'We like to play football that entertains the crowd – which is why we've replaced our goalie with a sea lion.'

'Mr Pochettino he say the lads do a good job, is a good three points and the interpreter he do such a fabulous job I double his wages.'

'I was very pleased with the way Rooney got a corner after only ten minutes. It's one of the most difficult eight-piece jigsaws I've ever seen.'

UNLIKELY THINGS TO HEAR
ON A NEWS PROGRAMME

'Now for a discussion on dementia. I'm joined
by Mrs Jones from the local retirement home
– and may I say what a nice nightie you're
wearing?'

'Nothing much has happened today, so here's
some music I wrote myself.'

'Before we go, just time to take a look at
tomorrow's papers: and here in the *Sun* we
can see that Caroline from Dagenham has
a smashing pair of norks.'

'Jeremy Bowen, in Damascus: could you
sum up the problems of the Middle East in
five seconds, please?'

'And for the latest on the norovirus that
is sweeping the BBC newsroom, we go to
Emily Maitlis in cubicle number 3.'

'In the headlines tonight, the Co-op bank
goes bust – sh*t, that's *my* bank!'

'And for the latest on that kitten stuck down
a well – it's dead. Good night.'

'Now we go to the centre of the riots in Egypt, where the reporter who pissed off the head of HR is standing.'

'As more western hostages are taken, it's over to our reporter on the spot, Bob Jackson . . . Bob? . . . Bob? . . . Bob!'

'The main headlines tonight: autocue operators call a wildcat str—'

'I'm not sure who won, but looking at the autocue, the scores were six minus four, three minus six, six minus two and six minus one.'

'We'll end the local news with a selection of viewers' photos . . . whoa! I think that's been sent to the wrong place.'

UNLIKELY THINGS TO READ
IN A MAINTENANCE MANUAL

No point checking the manual for this one; you'll just have to go to A&E and explain exactly what you've stuck into that Hoover.

Clean your sandwich toaster annually, or in other words: after every use.

First, remove cover from heating unit; look for sign saying 'Do not remove cover from heating unit, or your warranty will be invalidated'.

Your running treadmill should give years of trouble-free use once installed at the back of the wardrobe.

Using your new juicer, you'll soon discover how fresh, tasty and good value those supermarket juices really were.

No maintenance is required until someone falls out of the roller-coaster. Then you can tighten up the screws a bit.

Keep your maintenance manual in good condition at all times, as missing pages can be frustrating and especially dangerous if—

Wipe down surfaces with a cheap rag. The *Daily Mail* is best.

Before stripping the engine down, make sure you have a container handy to hold all the bits left over after you've rebuilt it.

THINGS YOU WOULDN'T HEAR IN
A HISTORY DOCUMENTARY

'And it was during this time that Britain was invaded by Anglo-Saxon tribes from Germany. The Saxons were highly sophisticated and intelligent, but the Angles were a bit obtuse.'

'On behalf of Channel 5, I'd like to apologize: it appears we've completely run out of stuff about Hitler.'

'It's fair to say that you couldn't have more information about Nazis if they'd won the war and programmed this channel themselves.'

'Coming up after the History Channel: the Geography Channel, the Double Chemistry Channel and the Free Period Channel.'

'Next: David Starkey discusses what an opinionated little tosspot he really is.'

'Coming up: *Nazi Atlantis* and *How Hitler Wanted to Rebuild the Pyramids*. You're watching the Not Really History Channel.'

'For centuries, people have pondered the mystery of why Stonehenge was built. Tonight, for the first time, we can reveal our vague guesswork at the answer.'

'Traditionally, Roman roads were built in dead straight lines – which is why, of course, Italians have never had to learn to drive properly.'

'The Austro-Hungarian Empire: a tough gig for any stand-up comedian.'

'If only King Harold had paid more attention to the name of his opponent, the chances of his being conquered might have been lower.'

'While Rome burned, Nero fiddled. And that's why he was later arrested by Operation Yewtree.'

'It was on this site that Cleopatra held an asp to her bosom – while Mark Antony winked and said, "Ey up, love, you need anyone to suck out the poison?"'

'I'm lying on an original guillotine, and if— "Cut!"'

'If Archduke Franz Ferdinand had not been assassinated, how different history would be. For example, the band Franz Ferdinand would have a different name.'

'With these stone benches and meagre rations, the ancient Greeks really did live a Spartan existence.'

'Do re-enactments really liven up a historical documentary? Well, I've come to Hastings to find – aaaargh, my eye! Who fired that f**king arrow?'

'It was here that Beethoven spent his final days, drooling and licking his genitals, chewing a bone and reflecting on the seven genuinely unfunny family films he had starred in.'

'It's amazing what we've learned from digging this one trench. We've learned that the local people get really pissed off when you drill through their electricity cable.'

'Despite not even having an O level in History, I'm determined to go back in time and find out more about Henry the Ninth.'

'And that's one theory about why Queen Victoria travelled alone: Prince Albert couldn't get through a metal detector without a lot of embarrassment.'

'Here is a design for the original *Mayflower* ship, destined for America. And you can see on the side here the warning, "Contents may settle".'

THINGS YOU WOULDN'T READ
IN A DIY MANUAL

There are only two things you need: duct tape and WD40.
If it moves and it shouldn't – use duct tape. If it doesn't move
and it should – use WD40.

Welcome to the *Reader's Digest Book of Ludicrously
Ambitious DIY Projects*. Chapter 1: A Floating Glass Gazebo.

This book is divided into two parts: projects that will take
months to complete, and projects that you'll never complete.

Then tighten the screws using a screwdriver – or in reality,
your thumbnail and a butter knife.

In order to maintain a professional standard, remember this
simple rule – righty tighty, lefty loosey.

Remember: the red wire is the live one. Or is it the yellow?
I can never remember.

The wires in the plug are earth, wind and fire . . . no, hang
on, that can't be right.

Don't forget the right tool belt. Put it on, and you'll look
like a right tool.

You will need one hammer, one screwdriver and one saw.
You are now ready to go and confront the men who did
your kitchen extension.

EXTRACTS FROM DVDS
THAT DIDN'T SELL

Always making poor decisions? Low self-esteem? You seem to be exactly the sort of loser who'd buy this kind of vacuous DVD.

Running, the Roger Bannister Way: Just watch this video, and you too will be able to run a mile exactly like an 85-year-old.

'I'm Paul Hollywood, and I'm going to be filling a variety of tarts. Let's hope my wife isn't watching!'

Welcome to *How to Stop Your Furniture from Wobbling*. Simply stick the DVD case under the wobbly leg, and it's problem solved!

'Hi, guys, and welcome to my new all-action video, all about how to be a Man's Man. Mum? Mum! Can you keep the noise down, I'm recording in here!'

'We're the Hairy Bikers, and we're going to show you how to make meals simply by foraging for free food we've found in our beards. Look . . . a leg of lamb, and most of a Scotch egg.'

Are you lacking confidence, and scared, when it comes to driving? Just do what I did – make a fortune from DVDs, and then you can afford a chauffeur to take you everywhere.

'Welcome to *How to Repair Your DVD Player*. Though I'm guessing you don't really need to watch this.'

BAD THINGS TO HEAR
YOUR NEW HOUSEMATE SAY

'Shall I bring my drums upstairs, or leave them downstairs by my bagpipes?'

'I'll probably only need the room for a couple of months . . . well, unless they find me not guilty.'

'I used to present a lot of entertainment shows on telly back in the Seventies, but I'm not so busy now.'

'I do have allergies, so if you could avoid leaving any bread, milk, cereal or meat in the kitchen that would be great.'

'I'll only need the spare room for a month or two, and then I guess we'll be getting married.'

'I already know what the bathroom's like – you can see right into it from the bushes in the back garden.'

'I'll happily do my share of cleaning the toilet, it's only fair – with my irritable bowel syndrome, I do make a hell of a mess.'

'I'm afraid it's not really working out with you sharing this house. You don't do any chores, or contribute in any way . . . a divorce is what I'm asking for.'

'When do I use the bathroom? Oh, pretty regularly – the first Tuesday of every month.'

'I only really need half a shelf in the fridge – just somewhere to store my stool samples for the doctor.'

UNLIKELY THINGS TO HEAR
ON CRIMEWATCH

'Two of the men then put stockings over their heads . . . I tell you, it was our best end-of-series party ever.'

'It seems the chainsaw murderer has struck again. The latest victim was found in the living room, the dining room and three of the bedrooms.'

'If you've been the victim of a sexual assault, you must report it. We won't take no for an answer.'

'As a detective, I try to get into the mind of a killer – by killing someone.'

'The victim was tied up and choked to death with four Weetabix. We're looking for a cereal killer.'

'Have you seen this man? He's a researcher at a TV studio, and I sent him off to get a cup of tea twenty minutes ago.'

'After being attacked, Mr Picasso sketched his assailant's face – but it's really not much help.'

'The speeding car was spotted several times along this stretch of road . . . oh, hang on, that's Silverstone.'

'Have you seen this man? You must have done – he was on *Top of the Pops* for the last thirty years.'

'That's it from me. Remember: don't have nightmares . . . aaah! Sorry – thought I saw a monster.'

'Do you recognize this man? If you said "Prince Andrew", there's a job for you in the Royal Protection Service.'

'Do you know the whereabouts of this fine life-size porcelain Dalmatian? If so, let us know – the bin men are coming tomorrow.'

'Have you seen this? It's a German fruit cake covered in marzipan and icing sugar. It's stollen.'

'The thieves broke into the post office at approximately 10.30, and reached the front of the queue just before lunchtime.'

'Don't forget, you can call Crimestoppers Anonymous in complete confidence. That's what Mrs Jones of 14 Henderson Avenue, Coventry did.'

'Remember: don't have nightmares. Just make sure you check under the bed and in the wardrobe for escaped killers.'

'They filled the lorry to the brim with goods from Lidl, and drove away with merchandise valued at nearly nine pounds.'

'This reconstruction recreates the events of that terrible night, but with slightly better-looking people.'

UNLIKELY THINGS TO HEAR
ON A CAR PROGRAMME

'This week, as an experiment, we've each selected a vehicle that directly corresponds to the size of our penis.'

'Before you lay out 200 grand for this car, bear in mind that you may not want to take the opinion of a man who still wears stonewashed denim in the year 2014.'

'Once again, I've traded up for a newer, sportier model. Yes, I've ditched Mrs Clarkson for a woman I met at work.'

'Today I'm testing this new electric car. Let's see how much juice it's got . . . oh, it's run out already.'

'This is the greenest car we've ever had on *Top Gear* – it is Bright Green.'

'This week's *Top Gear* will be shorter than usual, as we won't be using any lazy foreign stereotypes to describe the foreign cars. See you next week – good night!'

'This car was designed for the American market. It's got six cup holders, a sandwich stand, and a small rotisserie fitted to the dashboard.'

'If you don't have time to get a new in-car Christmas tree air freshener, simply get an ordinary piece of paper, write "I Stink" on it, and pop it on the dashboard.'

UNLIKELY THINGS TO HEAR
IN A SUPERHERO FILM

'Oh God, Spider-Man's stuck in the bath again! Get a mug
and an old postcard.'

'I'm not sure you've thought this disguise through properly,
have you, Badgerman?'

'Alright then, Iron Man, **you** do the ironing.'

'We'll go and save the world, Human Torch – you stay in the
cupboard under the stairs in case there's a power cut.'

'OK, Robin. Stand on the handle of that spade, and I'll take
some pictures for our Christmas cards.'

'I still don't see why, when I've got a house the size of
Wayne Mansion, I have to park the car in a f**king cave.'

'Run for it, AntMan! He's got a kettle!'

'One thing we've learned from this adventure, Robin:
we need talcum powder in the suit **before** we set off.'

'Bad news, Robin. While we were out, Catwoman's
sneaked in and shat in our slippers.'

UNLIKELY THINGS TO READ IN A PORN MAG

In this month's *Barely Legal*, we bring you the very best photos of our readers' worn and damaged car tyres and household cabling!

Shaved Wet Pussy: Enjoy Some of Britain's Cutest Bald Cats.

George, his face flushed, let out a long yelp of ecstasy, paused for breath and slowly got off. It had been the first time for ages, but it was everything he had hoped for. He wiped his arse, flushed the toilet and left.

'Give It to Me Hard Between My Legs' – Meet Suzy, 32, a superb player of fast bowling.

I got home last night to find my girlfriend had left a trail of photos leading to the bedroom. In each picture, she had removed one more thing. I found her on the bed, with no head, a torso and one remaining arm.

'I Want It Now in My Bathroom!' – How to Speak to Removal Men.

Talk to Hot Men NOW. Ask them whether it's the heating, or just you? Suggest opening a window, or maybe tinkering with the theromostat.

Inside This Month . . . oh, nothing, I don't know why we bloody bother. Why don't you just click on the Internet like everyone else?

Do you love massive dicks? Then meet 45-year-old Chris. He wears low-slung jeans and a baseball cap, goes to work on a scooter and pretends he likes rap music.

'16 and Sticky' – That's sixteen stickers for your Panini glamour girl sticker album *Tits 2014*, free inside.

See horny 'amateurs' as they cack-handedly attempt to pole dance and pleasure men like professionals!

'I Want You to Fill My Huge Crack' – Are you a plasterer? Can you help 42-year-old Doreen with the plastering in her utility room?

Meet Shaved Cougars NOW . . . at this shockingly cruel zoo in Kazakhstan. Help end the abuse of beautiful wild cats.

Readers' Wives: New Mingers Edition

Slowly, deliberately, she unpeeled the banana and put it in her mouth. She bit into it sexily. 'Like this?' she purred.

'Hmmm,' replied Frank. 'Well, you can eat a banana like that, I suppose, but it's a bit time-consuming. I just get it down in three big bites, luv.'

Hungrily, she unzipped his flies and reached inside. 'Can't find it. How f**king small are you?' she said unhappily.

This is Debbie. She likes reading, horses, cinema and politics; but mainly she likes creepy old men taking photos of her funbags for money (honest).

She stared at the member for what seemed an overly long time. Finally the silence was broken. The Right Honourable Jonathan Symes, MP had to get back to Parliament, and she still couldn't remember the question she wanted him to ask.

They went to bed. They had sex. He went downstairs and had a cup of tea with two sugars and watched *Question Time*.

She grabbed his trousers, and put her hand inside. 'Oh, you moron . . . this label says "dry clean only".'

'This is Babs, my twin sister. Have you ever done it with sisters before, Mr Brown?' she said, eyeing him suggestively as her sister edged closer to him on the couch.

'Not really,' he said. 'If I'm honest, I'm not much of a one for the sex stuff. Now, if you'll excuse me, I'm running late for a sales conference in Kettering.'

UNLIKELY PERSONAL ADS

Man with enormous cock would like to meet woman with large hen to discuss poultry farming.

Romantic man looking for fun relationship leading to marriage, with a view to reducing tax breaks.

Tall, dark professional footballer, Nobel Prize-winning scientist and ex-astronaut would like to meet beautiful, gullible woman.

Man with GSOH would like to meet woman with INW for winning hand at Scrabble.

Male, thirties, would like to meet . . . anyone. Apply J. Assange, Ecuadorian Embassy. Must enjoy staying in, short walks and discussions on liberty.

Ex-England footballer would like to meet someone else's wife.

21st-century metrosexual male seeks woman to cook and clean.

Elderly lady seeks man for companionship at home, so the cats don't eat me when I have a stroke.

Could YOU be the woman I'm looking for? Did YOU give me herpes in Tenerife six months ago?

Leader of Liberal Democrats, looking to meet male for dominant abusive relationship.

I'm tall, blonde and busty. I'd like to meet a doctor who can cure me of my man-boobs.

Is your partner just not into sex, like mine? Let's get together for a discreet affair. Contact Panda Enclosure, Edinburgh Zoo.

Guy seeks really tasty lady. Apply Hans the Cannibal, Pentonville.

Pinocchio seeks similar for relationship fun. No strings attached.

Heathcliff – it's me, Cathy. I'm not coming home.

Woman seeks man for help in slowly removing stockings. I can't bend down at my age, and these surgical ones are so tight when my ankles swell.

Fat, lonely man would like to hear from any girl at school who secretly fancied him. But will settle for a takeaway.

Gorgeous blonde woman with amazing body . . . would just like to let people know.

21-year-old girl, size 12, would like to meet a man who doesn't mind a woman with big feet.

BAD THINGS TO PUT IN AN
ELECTION MANIFESTO

Vote for us. There's no point explaining why; you're all too f**king stupid.

Well, if 'racist' means hating foreigners and anyone who isn't white, then . . . yeah, I guess we are pretty racist actually, thinking about it. Sorry.

For the last five years under David Cameron, the rich have got richer and the poor have got poorer . . . Great, isn't it? Vote Conservative.

Ed Balls is the man to lead Britain into a prosperous new – stop laughing.

Spend! Spend! Spend!

From now on, all Scots must wear a tartan hat of identification whenever they cross the border.

Attention, plebs! Time to vote.

Vote Llyr ap Rhydderch Evans Gruffydd, Your Plaid Cymru Candidate for Tunbridge Wells.

Vote for Me . . . and Get a Hand Job, Free.

I want to be your MP so that I can help you and our town – the town where I grew up – but mainly for the expenses, and the pussy.